Sunset
Ideas for
Hanging
Gardens

By the Editors of Sunset Books
and Sunset Magazine

Lane Publishing Co., Menlo Park, California

Foreword

If you're in the habit of viewing plants all growing at ground level, suspending a colorful plant can add a refreshingly new perspective to your garden. And don't overlook another advantage, too: with the help of hanging plants, the possibilities for decoration multiply dramatically.

For their advice, consultation, and generous help with this book, we thank Bob Bartholomew, Santa Ana, California; Naud Burnett, Dallas, Texas; Ed Carman, Los Gatos, California; James Griffin, Brandon, Florida; Ray Haines, Dallas, Texas; Donald H. Phillips, San Jose, California; Frank Prouty, Menlo Park, California; Wayne Roderick, Orinda, California; Daphne Smith, Los Altos, California; D. Don Spradlin, Palo Alto, California. And a special thanks to Ells Marugg, who worked closely with us on many special photography assignments.

Edited by Richard Osborne

Special Consultants: Joseph F. Williamson
Garden Editor
Sunset Magazine

Richard Dunmire,
Assistant Editor
Sunset Magazine

Design: Roger Flanagan

Illustrations: Dinah James

Front cover: Purple and yellow violas with
white sweet alyssum in wire baskets lend splashes of color to deck.
Photograph by William Aplin.

Back cover: Photograph by Glenn Christiansen.

Executive Editor, Sunset Books: David E. Clark

Third Printing December 1974

Contents

Special Features

Aerial Plants...
Freewheeling Fun

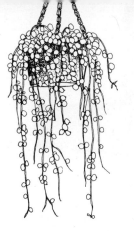

Immediately striking you with their dazzling flowers, graceful foliage, and dramatic form, plants suspended in the air take on a special perspective: they are showpieces in the round.

In growing hanging plants, you follow most of the basic techniques used in container gardening on the ground. You also have a wide selection of different kinds of plants, containers, and hangers to choose from.

By no means are you limited to a group of plants that have been officially designated as airborne. You can

Piggy-back plant
(*Tolmiea menziesii*)

Boston fern
(*Nephrolepis exaltata*
'Bostoniense')

Nemesia (*N. strumosa*)

use landscape and specimen shrubs, perennials, succulents, tropicals, ferns, annuals, and even such fruiting plants as strawberries and cherry tomatoes. The most popular hanging plants have long trailing stems that will form a lovely cascade of foliage or flowers.

Hanging plants offer a fresh, unique approach to gardening that is highly conducive to freewheeling innovation. You can suspend almost any plant that will grow in a container and is not too large or upright. For an adventure, try hanging your container of planted bulbs, a bonsai specimen, or even a terrarium. Small bedding plants packed into the sides of a moss-lined wire basket will provide a living bouquet of color. Arrangements of several different plants in the same container can become a small landscape in the air.

The fascination of a hanging container will enhance even a baby plant purchased at the dimestore. Some who are attracted to hanging gardens consider the plant almost secondary and choose one of the many fine and attractively designed containers as the main emphasis for their display.

But hanging plants aren't just a novelty. To many plant lovers, especially to those confined to small living quarters, the air provides a fine home for plants that will free valuable ground or floor space.

In addition to saving space, hanging plants provide a convenient solution to many landscape and interior decoration problems. They can soften harsh surfaces of walls, define walkways and living areas, and fill empty corners.

Whether you begin with one or two purchased on a Saturday afternoon lark or a dozen exotic specimens, and whether you grow them indoors or out, hanging plants will give you a delightful little garden overhead.

Outdoors the possibilities are many

If you consider the air as a gardening place, you realize that a hanging garden can give you the equivalent space of a new border or even a second backyard. All you need is an overhead support from which to hang plants and a sense of fun and adventure.

Points to consider before hanging a plant

Think about these factors when choosing a location for a hanging plant: the strength of the supporting structure; the location's exposure to such elements as sun, shade, and wind; and the convenience of the location for you.

Provide a strong supporting structure. The structure you choose must be strong enough to support both your plant and container. The weight of a container full of soil and plants can be considerable: a 12-inch wooden box or wire basket, for example, can weigh as much as 30 pounds, even more after watering. An overhanging beam that holds up the roof of your house,

supports for a patio structure, or a tree limb that's thick and sturdy enough to hold the threaded end of a screw hook should be strong enough to support almost any container and plant. Be cautious when suspending a container, especially a large one, from thin roofing or exterior facades that aren't actually a part of the structural framework of a building. And test tree limbs for their strength and flexibility before you adorn them with plants.

Estimate sun, shade, and wind exposure. Because different plants require varying amounts of sun, shade, and heat, it's advisable to choose the location before selecting the plant. Then, after checking the spot every few hours during the day to see how much sun and shade it receives, choose a plant that thrives under these conditions. On pages 10-14 you'll find suggestions for full sun, shade, and part sun/part shade plants. You might pick one of these if you don't already have a plant in mind. Or study the plant lists on pages 44-78 or ask your nurseryman for other suggestions.

If, like many shoppers, you've succumbed to the temptation of a spur-of-the-moment plant purchase, look up the plant on pages 44-78 or ask a nurseryman or experienced green thumber what conditions it likes and then try to find a location that best suits its needs.

In addition to making certain your location will provide the proper amounts of sun and shade for the plant you'd like to grow, check to see that it isn't exposed to reflected heat or strong winds. Walls and fences, particularly those painted a light color, can reflect the sun's rays and greatly increase their intensity, even burning or wilting specimens that tolerate direct sunlight. Locations not protected by fences and

As traditional as mounted police: *Wire baskets adorn lampposts in Canadian city of Victoria.*

Patio roofs *are ideal for hanging plants. Here, begonias and fuchsias luxuriate in gentle shade.*

Wandering Jew *in a metal wall bracket brings life to this otherwise bare location.*

In a shady breezeway, *grape ivy (left, right), plectranthus (center) balance border plants.*

This spider plant *is framed by an opening in a garden wall that also provides light shade.*

Magnificently trailing *plectranthus welcomes guests through shaded entryway.*

walls may be subject to winds that will rapidly dry out a plant and possibly disturb or break pendant stems or even knock the plant down.

Choose a convenient location. Perhaps most immediately important to you is a location that is pleasing and convenient. Your personal tastes are the best guide in choosing an attractive location, but several tips might help you choose one that's convenient.

• Try to avoid locations where your hanging plant would be in the way of traffic or block a view. Just brushing your shoulder against some plants is enough to damage their leaves or flowers and perhaps even break delicate stems. If you or your guests happen to bump a plant severely, its container can give a lump on the head. Plants normally out of the way except when you're puttering underneath them can be especially irksome—forgetting they are overhead, you can stand up quickly and bump them.

• Water dripping from baskets and drainage holes in some pots and boxes is another inconvenience, especially if the plant is hanging above a carpet or patio surface that stains easily or is difficult to clean. Delicate shrubs can also be damaged by floods of water gushing from an overhead container. One easy solution is to use an undrained container (see page 18). Another is to take the plant down when you water. Or suspend a drip saucer beneath the container. (See page 34 for more information on the drip problem.)

• Considerations of height and ease of hanging a plant might also enter into your choice of a location, but they should not play too great a role. As long as a structure is higher than the level at which you want the plant to hang, you can adjust its height by lengthening or shortening the hanger. Wooden structures into which you can easily screw a hook or supports that you can loop a hanger around are often the easiest from which to hang a plant. But, with just a bit more effort, you can also use brick, concrete, or stucco structures if you follow the proper techniques (See pages 36-37.)

Choosing an outdoor support for hanging plants

Once you begin to think in terms of suspended gardens, you can range widely in locating an overhead support. A tree in a garden, an overhang, or a patio shelter might be suitable. You might even build a special frame just for a hanging garden.

Here are some suggestions for outdoor supports from which you may like to suspend a plant:

Overhangs. A roof edge extending out from a wall far enough to let a plant dangle freely is an excellent location for hanging plants. Try to utilize beams underneath the overhanging roof, for they usually have the most strength. If the beams aren't exposed or convenient and the container is not a heavy one, try hanging it from the subroofing. But be sure it's sturdy enough to give the hook or eye screw a good bite and strong enough to offer the necessary support for the container's weight.

Check for possible conditions of extreme sun and shade during different parts of the day beneath the overhang and watch for reflected heat from nearby walls. Also look for borders beneath the overhang that might make for difficult access to the plant for watering and care.

The effects you can create by hanging plants from overhangs are many. Often stark and bare, walls and corners beneath overhangs can be softened and given texture by a row of hanging plants. Hung at the same

Along a walkway, *plants suspended from roof overhang complement border, screen windows.*

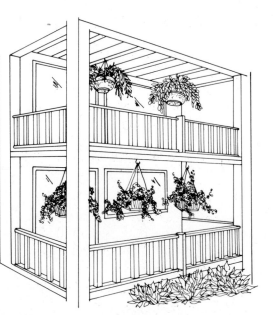

Apartment terraces *gain privacy and color from hanging plants without sacrificing floor space.*

level, plants reinforce a formal or structured atmosphere. Dangling at different heights, they give a feeling of movement and informality.

One or two plants suspended outside a window can create a nice framing effect, provide a natural screen, or offer an attractive view from inside the house.

Overhangs often extend beyond the edge of an apartment terrace. There, hanging plants can effectively screen off the terrace and provide a feeling of privacy and seclusion.

Entries and porches. Suspended from the roof or overhang above an entry or porch, plants offer your guests a pleasant welcome, fill unsightly corners, frame a door or window, or counterbalance shrub borders or plants in ground-level containers.

Patio structures. Does your patio have a shade roof or other type of overhead structure? In addition to a roof overhang, a patio shelter or other garden structure (such as a lath house or gazebo) is an ideal place from which to hang plants. If you use such a structure, make sure that your plants don't interrupt traffic patterns or create unnecessary obstacles.

Above the patio or terrace, hanging plants can divide large areas to create small spaces that have a private, intimate atmosphere. At the edge of a patio, they'll separate it more distinctly from the garden by forming a casual screen.

Near posts or patio walls, one or two hanging plants can quietly soften lines and corners of a structure by filling otherwise barren spaces. Centered boldly between two vertical supports of a patio roof, one pendent plant becomes an eye-catching focal point; two or three might frame a prized garden view or invite you down a garden path.

Framing this front door *are two spider plants. In cold climates they move indoors for the winter.*

Give your bulbs a lift

Perhaps heretical to the traditional gardener—but intriguing to freewheelers—are bulbs in the air. They really prove that almost any plant will hang as long as it isn't too large or upright. Dwarf varieties under 12 inches tall are most suitable. Plant them as you normally would in a pot or box. When bloom begins, suspend the container at about waist or chest height so non-trailing flowers will be visible.

Following are a few bulbs you can try:

BEGONIA. For many types and varieties, see pages 44–78.

CROCUS. Suspend your crocus jar in a decorative sling.

CYCLAMEN. Mass them into the sides of a basket or use them in a pot or box.

HYACINTH. Use short types. Plant in a shallow pot, bowl, or box. See photo, page 76.

LACHANELIA. Flower stalks lean over container's sides.

ORNITHOGALUM CAUDATUM. Pregnant onion. Exotic house plant; see pages 44–78.

TULIP. Dwarf varieties are best. Plant in a shallow pot, bowl, or box.

Trees. As long as they are strong enough not to bend or break under the weight of a container, horizontal branches of trees make ideal supports. The effect can be quite pleasing: a casual, informal garden touched with leisurely variety. And many trees provide even, well-lighted shade that's not always available beneath overhangs and patio roofs. To hang a plant from a tree limb, use a hook or eye screw in the branch.

Walls, fences, and posts. If you don't have a convenient overhead structure, you can always hang your plants against a wall, fence, or post. Though they may not have the appeal of plants swinging freely, they will still be at eye level and will soften and give character to flat surfaces and rigid lines. Be cautious of reflected sunlight from walls and fences. You may want to read through the sections on containers and methods of hanging plants to find the most suitable container for a wall and how to hang it.

Choosing a plant to hang outdoors

Giving advice on choosing a hanging plant is similar to helping you select clothing: there are many possibilities, and your choice ultimately will depend on your personal taste and on what will be appropriate for the setting.

Generally, plants with long, trailing stems are favored for hanging, but feel free to experiment with almost any container plant except those that are large and upright. A number of plants that are attractive in hanging containers are described on pages 44-78.

Outdoor possibilities (cont'd.)

Some are attractive foliage plants, whereas others have magnificent blossoms. Don't feel you're limited only to this list; if you see a plant you like at the nursery or plant shop that looks as though it might be attractive when suspended, try it out. (If you have doubts about its ability to hang, ask the nurseryman for advice.)

The one factor you must consider when choosing any plant is culture. Since different plants require different amounts of sun, shade, light, and heat, be sure the plant you select will take to the conditions peculiar to the location you've chosen.

Below are lists of plants for full sun, shade, and part sun/part shade. Intended as suggestions only, the lists are not meant to limit your choice but rather to give you a starting point.

Defining in hard terms the conditions that constitute full sun, shade, and part sun/part shade and then classifying plants as absolutely belonging to one group or another is difficult. Full sun, especially if reflected by a wall or fence, can be much hotter in the desert, for example, than in a coastal area. Shade can have an intensity of light ranging from extremely bright to very low. Then, too, many plants will tolerate some amounts of shade or sun as long as they receive enough of their preferred exposure.

Plants for full sun. In general, a location in full sun is one that receives direct sunlight most of the day, particularly during the hot mid-afternoon. But direct sun can be more intense in some climates than in others, and sun can also be much hotter when reflected by a wall or fence. If you live in a very warm climate, where summer afternoon temperatures average above 75°, or if your location receives reflected sunlight, watch your plant carefully for the first few weeks to see that it doesn't suffer from burning or wilting from too much sun or heat. If a plant does show signs of burn or wilt, make certain it has adequate water and move it to a location of less intense sun, perhaps one that provides direct sun most of the day but light shade during the hottest afternoon hours.

The following are plants you might try in locations exposed to direct sun.

Amaracus dictamnus (Crete dittany). Herb grown for flowers and foliage. Full sun.

Calceolaria integrifolia. Provide light shade during hottest part of the day in warm climates.

Convolvulus mauritanicus (Ground morning glory). Good bloom in dry heat.

Euonymus fortunei 'Gracilis'. Takes full sun as well as shade; grown for foliage, texture.

Herbs take to altitude

Hanging in a kitchen window or outside the kitchen door, a pot of herbs offers tasty flavors to your cooking and is a study in foliage texture as well. Just plant several in a pot, putting the upright growers (parsley and chives, primarily) in the center. Most herbs like full or partial sun and moist, well-drained soil. Regularly snip off leaves to keep plants full and bushy.

Here are some favorites you can hang:

BASIL. Use the leaves in salads or with fish, poultry, eggs.

CHIVES. Snip or chop the long, grasslike leaves into salads, eggs for a mild onion flavor.

MARJORAM. The small leaves go well with meats, salads, casseroles. Keep flowers trimmed off.

MINT. Fresh fragrant leaves. Likes partial shade.

OREGANO. Flavor like marjoram but stronger. Use in Italian and Spanish dishes. Keep flowers trimmed off.

PARSLEY. Upright stems topped by leaves you can use as garnish or in salads, vegetables.

ROSEMARY. Leaves are tasty in meats, stews. Use small varieties. See pages 44–78.

SAGE. Use the gray green leaves to season meat, cheese, poultry.

SAVORY. Leaves of either the perennial or annual savory are good with meats, fish, eggs, vegetables.

TARRAGON In salads, in egg and cheese dishes, and with fish, the leaves add distinctive flavor.

THYME. Use the leaves with fish, meat, salads. See pages 44–78.

Culinary garden *in a strawberry jar: pockets hold basil, marjoram, thyme; chives, parsley fill top.*

Gazania, trailing types. Daisylike flowers; takes full sun.

Lantana montevidensis. Tends to mildew in shade or continued overcast.

Lotus. (See species, page 62.) Can stand reflected heat.

Mahernia verticillata. Spring flowers. Needs good drainage, full sun.

Oscularia deltoides, trailing types (Ice plant). Tolerates dry heat.

Osteospermum fruticosum (Trailing African daisy). Good winter and spring bloom for sunny locations in mild climates.

Petunia. Many want light shade during afternoon in hot climates.

Portulaca grandiflora. Flowers open fully only in sun, close late afternoon.

Sedum sieboldii. Tough, spreading succulent for fall bloom. Sun or light shade.

Senecio confusus (Mexican flame vine). Will take light shade as well as sun; keep soil moist.

Thunbergia alata (Black-eyed Susan vine). Annual flower for summer bloom in sunny locations.

Plants for shady locations. Just as sunny garden locations can vary considerably in temperature and intensity, so can shady spots. Some shady locations, especially those along north or east walls or in narrow areas between a fence and a wall, may be densely shaded, whereas locations under high branching trees are often very light with only thin shade perhaps broken or streaked by sunlight. In addition to not getting enough light, shady spots in cool climates may not offer enough heat for otherwise shade-loving plants. In the desert, on the other hand, the same amount of shade can be almost unbearably hot for shade-loving plants.

Some plants will thrive in constant deep shade with very little light, but others will become rangy in these conditions as they stretch out for light. Their flowers may be small and discolored from lack of light. If your plants in the shade are growing with sparse foliage on long rangy stems or the flowers don't open fully, try moving them to a brighter location. In hot climates, watch your shade plants to see if they are wilting from intense heat, just as you would if they were in direct sun or were exposed to reflected heat. If wilting occurs, move them to a cooler location.

In cool and humid areas, many otherwise shade-loving plants might be grown in the sun as long as they are protected and well watered when hot spells do occur.

The following are plants you might try in shady areas of the garden.

Chlorophytum comosum (Spider plant). Semi-tropical, moisture-loving plant. Protect from frosts. Bring indoors during winter.

Cissus rhombifolia (Grape ivy). Takes low light intensity but needs year-round warmth; indoor/outdoor plant.

Cymbalaria muralis (Kenilworth ivy). Moisture

Rattan hanger *holds an asparagus fern in a ramada entrance, where it receives protection, light shade.*

and steady shade with good light. Indoor/outdoor plant in harsh climates.

Epiphyllum (Orchid cactus). Broken shade under trees, lath; protect from frost.

Euonymus fortunei 'Gracilis'. Takes sun as well as full shade.

Ferns. Most prefer humidity and need protection from frosts (see cultures, pages 44-78). The following ferns are fine for a tropical effect on a shady patio: *Davallia, Nephrolepis* (Boston fern), *Pellaea, Polypodium, Pyrrosia.*

Lysimachia nummularia (Creeping Jennie). Moisture and even shade.

Mimulus tigrinus. Grow in shade, perhaps with ferns, primroses.

Nemesia strumosa. Light shade or filtered sun.

Plectranthus. (See species, page 67.) Same culture as grape ivy; stands very low light intensity.

Rhoeo spathacea. Takes low or high light intensity, casual watering.

Saxifraga stolonifera (Strawberry geranium). Light shade.

(Continued on page 14)

Fairy primrose (*Primula malacoides*)

Hanging plants in the garden

Summer flowers in wall baskets

Frequently, hanging plants are just a bit of Saturday afternoon fun. On your next jaunt to the nursery, pick up some small flowering plants to hang from a tree limb, like the fairy primroses above. Or choose a variety of flowers and set them in wire baskets. They'll grace a walkway when suspended from an overhang. For a more permanent display, select an evergreen plant. Dangle one in front of a window—like the donkey tail sedum (facing page)—you'll enjoy it both indoors and out.

If you can't find a convenient tree or overhang for your plant, use wall mounting baskets or boxes. The wall at right is literally alive with bloom, and valuable patio space hasn't been sacrificed. Another idea for garden fancy is a wooden frame adorned with plants. The one on the facing page uses 4 by 4s for upright supports, 2 by 2s for cross pieces.

Donkey tail sedum (*Sedum morganianum*)

Mixed flowers in wire baskets

Cascade petunias

Bonsai: style in the air

Steeped in tradition, the art of bonsai offers combined rewards of gardening and creating natural art forms. Bonsai plants are sometimes sold at nurseries, or you can establish a plant yourself. Either way, have you thought of hanging your bonsai? It will bring the plant right up to eye level where its form—its most important aspect—can easily be seen. Just use a sling-type hanger that will complement the bonsai container and the plant's shape. Many books on bonsai are available at bookstores and libraries. From these, you can learn bonsai techniques and discover which plants might be used.

Bonsai juniper *hangs slightly below chest level where its graceful branches are seen and appreciated.*

(Continued from page 11)

Schizocentron elegans (Spanish shawl). Protect from frost.

Vinca. (See species, page 78.) Best in shade with moisture but will take part sun if generously watered.

Part sun/part shade plants. Many garden locations, especially those facing east or west or those near walls or fences, are exposed to bright sun in the morning and deep shade in the afternoon (or the other way around). Generally, morning sun and afternoon shade provide a stable balance of temperature, offering warm sun in the cool morning and protection from direct sun in the hot afternoon. Locations exposed to morning shade and long afternoon hours of direct sun, particularly if near a reflecting wall or fence, may often be comparable to those with full sun. Other part sun/part shade conditions are those with shade interrupted by streaks or spots of sunlight filtering through tree limbs or through a lath shelter.

Try these plants in part sun/part shade locations:

Abutilon megapotamicum. Afternoon or partial shade in warmer climates to full or afternoon sun in coastal and other cool locations.

Asparagus, ornamental. (See species, page 46.) Foliage is greenest in bright, sun-filtered shade or in morning sun and light afternoon shade.

Browallia. (See species, page 48.) Light sun or filtered shade.

Campanula. Good light, partial shade.

Coleus. Best foliage color in good indirect light. Stands some sun or shade but leaf color won't be as bright.

Impatiens walleriana. Part shade, moisture.

Lobelia erinus. Morning sun, light afternoon shade.

Loropetalum chinense. Full sun in cool areas, partial shade elsewhere.

Pelargonium. (See species, page 65.) Good light, partial shade.

Rosmarinus (Rosemary). See species, page 71. Endures hot afternoon sun and morning or late afternoon shade; also grown in warm shade dappled with sunlight.

Sedum morganianum (Donkey tail sedum). Light shade.

Tropaeolum majus (Nasturtium). Best in sun or good light but will stand periods of shade.

Hanging plants indoors

The ceiling and walls of your house or apartment offer excellent supports from which to hang your house plants, especially specimens with trailing or spreading stems. Besides being attractive, hanging plants indoors can fill awkward corners and add a garden feeling to any room. Hanging against a wall, they're an alternative to framed paintings or prints.

If the ceiling of your house or apartment is unfinished, has exposed beams, or is paneled with strong wood, you can probably just screw a hook into it wherever convenient and hang up the plant. However, many ceilings, especially in apartments, are made of gypsum board or plaster over lath which alone will not offer the resiliency of wood in clenching the threads of a screw securely enough to prevent it from pulling loose. You can, of course, try screwing the hook right into the plaster or gypsum board (drill a small pilot hole first) and, if your container is only a small one, the hook may hold. But don't count on this happening. Just bumping the plant while watering may be enough to knock it down. You're much better off locating a ceiling joist (usually wooden 2 by 6s or 2 by 8s) beneath the plaster or gypsum board and, after carefully drilling a pilot hole, screwing in a hook that's long enough to penetrate the ceiling material and joist. If you want to hang a plant from a wall covered with gypsum board or plaster, find a wall stud beneath the covering and screw the hook into it.

To find a ceiling joist or wall stud, measure 14½ inches out from a major corner. The other joists or studs should fall every 16 inches. (On some buildings they are 20 or 24 inches apart.) Keep in mind that joists run in one direction only, so measure from the corner

East-facing *kitchen window will provide morning sun, indirect light in the afternoon, just right for many tender plants that spend the winter indoors.*

Sturdy towel *rack easily lets you swing plants into or out of the sun from a window.*

Even small apartments *have room for plants in the air. Here are philodendrons, wandering Jew (center).*

Open hallway *gains a lanai atmosphere from hanging plants.*

Boston ferns *give this airy, well-lighted kitchen a graceful finishing touch.*

along both walls to be sure to locate one. Studs run up and down a wall.

Other methods of locating covered framework are to use a stud finder (a magnetic device available in hardware stores) or to knock firmly on the ceiling or wall with the heel of your fist. A solid sound means you've located a joist or stud; a hollow sound should tell you to keep looking.

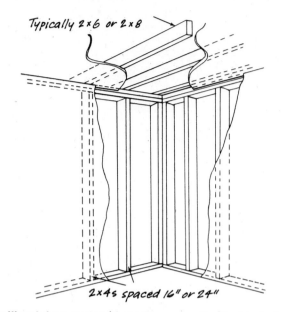

Typically 2×6 or 2×8

2×4s spaced 16" or 24"

Ceiling joists and wall studs *are located behind plaster or gypsum board, offer best support. Find them by measuring or tapping on the wall or ceiling.*

If finding a joist or stud is inconvenient or you can't locate one where you'd like the plant to hang, try using plastic or lead "sleeves" available at hardware stores. Inserted into a drilled hole, the sleeve expands to create a binding fit when you screw a hook into it. Expansion bolts, also available at hardware stores, are another helpful device.

Further tips and technical information on using such hardware as hooks, sleeves, and spreading fasteners are on pages 36-37.

Where you locate your plant indoors will depend on convenience, personal taste, and the needs of the plant. Remember to avoid locations where the plant would be an obstacle to traffic and to use an undrained container or hang a drip saucer beneath a pot with a drain hole.

Following are tips on providing the right culture for an indoor plant.

Indoor locations

All plants require some light. Windows are favored locations for house plants because they provide good light. (Fluorescent lamps are usually impractical and unattractive when hung above or around pendent plants.)

Ideally, north-facing windows (unless shaded by trees or buildings outside) provide good, even light throughout the day but not direct sun. Windows facing east or west offer intense light or even direct sun in the morning or afternoon and less light during other parts of the day.

South-facing windows generally receive the most intense sunlight for the greatest part of the day. Before locating a plant in or near a window that receives direct sun, be sure it won't burn or wilt from the heat. If you want the good light of a sunny window but know your plant won't tolerate direct sun, hang it off to the side of the window. Pale foliage on the plant may indicate it's receiving too much light.

For your own convenience, hang plants far enough away from windows so they won't be an inconvenience when you open and close draperies. In a sunny window, the foliage may become scorched if it touches the hot pane.

Locations away from windows, in a room's interior, may or may not provide enough light for your plant. Generally speaking, a location that has enough indirect light for you to read comfortably for an hour or two without turning on a lamp should also provide enough light for most house plants. Do watch your plant, though, for signs of spindly growth or dropping leaves that may indicate inadequate light. In dark corners or other locations that receive low light intensity, try such plants as grape ivy (*Cissus rhombifolia*) and plectranthus, which do well in weak light.

Most house plants prefer even temperatures and resent wide fluctuations between night and day. Try to avoid placing them in locations exposed to cool drafts of chilly air. Be sure windows near plants are shut tight during the night if temperatures drop more than 10 or 15 degrees. Hang your plants far enough away from heat sources and appliances that may toast or dry them out.

Plants to hang indoors

Among the many house plants that are available at nurseries, florist shops, plant boutiques, and even some supermarkets, many will hang and dangle attractively. In general, the kinds of plants best suited to hang indoors are tropical or semi-tropical or do well with little or no direct sunlight. Many indoor plants are indoor/outdoor specimens that grow well on the patio or in another sheltered outdoor location during the warm months but are brought inside for protection from the cold during the winter.

In selecting an indoor hanging plant, consider the conditions of your house, where you'd like the plant to grow—in a bright window or in a dark corner—and how much time you'd like to spend taking care of it. Some plants, such as fittonia, require high humidity and constant warmth; others, such as coleus, need even light; still others, such as achimenes, need a warmer or cooler temperature than is comfortable for people. You can, of course, regulate indoor growing

Hanging terrariums and miniature gardens

Fascinating arrangements of plants in small bowls, dishes, jars, and bottles, terrariums and miniature gardens take on added interest when suspended from the ceiling. Some commercial terrarium and dish garden containers are designed for hanging, but for others, a bit of ingenuity might devise a sling-type hanger that will work.

Technically, a terrarium is a closed environment—a bottle or jar with a lid. Inside is an atmosphere of high humidity and warmth. Tropical plants that thrive in such conditions are best: maranta, ferns, pilea, syngonium, and ivy are just a few. Select your plants to create an interesting study in texture and foliage color. Use small specimens growing in 3 or 4-inch containers.

For creating miniature gardens in open containers (such as dishes or bonsai pots), you can use a much wider selection of small plants than just those that like humidity and moisture. Since your goal is to create a miniature landscape, you might include in the arrangement such items as driftwood, an interesting rock, or gravel. Because you should look down into a dish garden as much as you look at it from the side, hang it low, perhaps slightly above waist level.

For more information on the culture, planting, and care of terrariums and miniature gardens, refer to one of the many books about them at bookstores, nurseries, or the library.

Suspended wood and glass terrarium *houses such moisture lovers as spathiphyllum, syngonium, pilea.*

conditions by adjusting the thermostat, spraying the plant with a water mister to creater high humidity, or setting it in a proper window.

Below are listings of plants that are relatively easy to grow indoors. In general, these plants do well in the warm, dry conditions of many homes. (For further information on each, see pages 44-78.)

Aechmea. Bromeliad; provide good air circulation.

Asparagus, ornamental. (See species, page 46.) Foliage color and growth best in strong, indirect light.

Ceropegia woodii (Rosary vine). Succulent that will stand a sunny window and/or good, indirect light.

Chlorophytum comosum (Spider plant). Grows best in fully lighted window.

Cissus rhombifolia (Grape ivy). Tolerates low light intensity; place in corners, windowless entries.

Coleus. Colors show up best in strong, indirect light.

Davallia trichomanoides. Requires good indirect light.

Ficus pumila (Creeping fig). Tolerates medium-low light.

Humata tyermannii (Bear's foot fern). Likes good, indirect light.

Maranta leuconeura (Prayer plant). Grow in warm north light.

Nephrolepis exaltata 'Bostoniense' (Boston fern). Lovely, very popular fern. North light in a cool room suits it best. Spray fronds regularly with water for humidity in dry rooms.

Peperomia. (See species, page 66.) Grow in north light.

Philodendron. Good light but avoid direct sun through a window.

Pilea. (See species, page 67.) Prefers temperatures between 65° and 70°; good light.

Plectranthus. (See species, page 67.) Tolerates low light intensity.

Rhaphidophora aurea. The same conditions as philodendron.

Rhoicissus capensis (Evergreen grape). Tolerates low light.

Schlumbergera bridgesii (Christmas cactus). Winter bloom; provide strong light or sun from window.

Senecio mikanioides (German ivy). Likes good, even light.

Syngonium podophyllum. The same culture as philodendron.

Container Know-How

When you shop for a plant to hang, you'll find many already growing in suspended containers. For an immediate display, all you have to do is buy one of these, take it home, and hang it up.

But don't limit your search to plants already suspended. Growing at ground level in ordinary pots, cans, or flats are many plants that would make excellent hanging specimens if replanted into more suitable containers and given time to fill out.

Buying your plant and container separately gives you a much wider choice of plants than just those the nursery has featured as hangers. Descriptions of plants you might want to try in the air appear in chapter 5 on pages 44-78. Below is a discussion of different types of containers and how to plant in them.

Containers for hanging plants

A wire basket lined with sphagnum moss is the classic hanging container. It's the kind of container shown on this book's cover. Certainly it is attractive, especially when planted with masses of flowers around the sides. But by no means is a basket the only type of container you can hang. Commercially made clay and plastic pots and wooden boxes are often used; they can be found along with baskets at nurseries and garden supply centers.

More unusual containers, such as hand-thrown clay pots, sculpted wooden boxes, leaded glass planters, and unique imported and specialty designs, are available at some nurseries and plant boutiques. You might also find a container by browsing through hand-craft and ceramic shops, import stores, and craft fairs.

Something truly original—a lettuce or woven basket (be sure it's strong enough), wire birdcage, plastic pith helmet, or an attractive mixing bowl from the kitchen—might also serve as a container.

Choosing a container

Pots, boxes, or baskets—all containers do the same basic job of holding your plant and its roots. The type you choose is really a matter of your plant's needs and your own personal tastes and preferences. The following considerations should help you make the most satisfactory choice: the container's hangability, size, porosity, and drainage.

Hangability. Remember the proverbial sailor who built his boat in the basement only later to realize that he couldn't get it out? Don't put yourself in a similar position by getting a container that won't easily hang.

Baskets and many commercial pots and boxes are designed specifically for hanging and have holes or hooks in their rim to accommodate a number of different manufactured and homemade hangers. Some even come with the hanger as a part of their design. But for others that aren't meant for hanging, you may have to improvise a special hanger.

Plant hangers, both commercial and homemade, are discussed and illustrated on pages 32-36. You'll be wise to browse through this section to get an idea of the ways you might suspend your container before actually buying one. If possible, purchase the hanger and container together.

Size. Most commercial containers come in small, medium, and large sizes. A good rule is to get one an inch or two larger in diameter than the plant's nursery container. For baskets, allow an additional 2 or 3 inches for the moss lining (see page 27).

For plants in 1-gallon cans, use about an 8 or 9-inch pot or box or a 12 to 14-inch basket. Use a 12 to 14-inch pot or a 14 to 16-inch basket for plantings that involve two or three 1-gallon can plants.

Keep in mind that 12-inch containers may weigh 30 pounds or more, 14 and 16-inch sizes up to 50 or 60 pounds. You'll probably find 8 to 12-inch containers the most useful and easiest to hang.

Porosity. Though many materials are used to make plant containers, most fall into one of two categories: porous or nonporous. Porous containers include untreated wooden boxes, unglazed clay pots, and moss-lined baskets, all of which allow air and moisture to reach the soil. Nonporous containers—glazed clay, plastic, and metal pots and some treated or lined wooden boxes, for example—prevent air and moisture from penetrating.

What all this means to you as a gardener is that the soil in a porous container will dry out more quickly than it will in a nonporous type. Consequently you'll have to water a plant in a porous container more frequently than the same plant growing in a nonporous one.

Drainage. If allowed to collect in the bottom of a container, water that isn't absorbed immediately by the soil can rot the roots or drown a plant. Some containers have a hole in the bottom to allow excess water to run out. Though this is an excellent solution to the drainage problem, it creates another: drip that can stain a patio surface, ruin a carpet, and, perhaps most annoying, give you an unexpected shower. Wire baskets and unlined wooden boxes are especially notorious for sloppy drainage.

On page 39, several solutions to the drip problem are discussed. One is to use a container (most often a pot) without drainage holes. Another is to suspend a drip saucer beneath the container to collect excess water. If you do use an undrained container, be sure to take the extra step of adding layers of sand and charcoal to the bottom before planting. (See planting instructions, page 24.) Take precautions as noted on page 38 not to water undrained containers excessively.

If you find a pleasing container that doesn't have a drainage hole, drill one yourself. In an average-sized container (about 8 to 12 inches in diameter), make one ½-inch hole in the bottom. Use an electric or hand drill for a wooden box or plastic pot. In clay and ceramic pots, drill the hole with a carbide bit in an electric drill, supporting the pot on a sturdy block of wood. Be careful to work slowly to prevent cracking. A little water in the bottom of the pot should make drilling easier.

Some clay pots have a knock-out drain hole that appears as a slight indentation—all you do is lightly tap out the disk of clay.

Pots

Clay, ceramic, and plastic pots are the container gardener's mainstay. Available at virtually every nursery and garden center, they come in a wide range of shapes, styles, designs, and sizes, some with drainage holes, some without. Some are made specifically for hanging and come with holes in the rim or even a hanger. Others may not be intended for the air but can be given a lift if you design a hanger for them.

Probably most familar are the traditional terra cotta pots. Brick red, their standard color, will enhance any plant you may have, either indoors or out. Some manufacturers also offer them in cream, tan, brown, and black.

Glazed ceramic pots, somewhat more decorative than the unglazed types, are especially suitable for indoor plants. The glaze gives a nonporous finish in colors that often vary with the manufacturer but usually include white, blue, green, yellow, red, brown, and black, as well as mottled and streaked colors and textures. Be sure to select a color that complements the foliage and flowers of your plant.

Don't shun plastic pots just because they may not seem as traditional and natural as clay or wooden containers, for these actually have several advantages over their cousins. Lightweight yet extremely durable, plastic pots won't easily crack or break. Nonporous, they retain moisture far better than even glazed clay pots. Inexpensive, plastic pots are available in an ever-growing range of designs and in colors that run a rainbow gamut—white and green being very popular and more versatile than some of the others. You might enjoy the novelty of clear plastic types that display the soil and roots.

When using plastic pots, be careful to plant in a light soil and avoid overwatering. Plastic is nonporous, and plants whose roots like plenty of air—the Boston fern, for instance—may suffer from the limited entry of air

(Continued on page 22)

Available at most nurseries *(clockwise from top): Plastic pot with clip-on drip saucer, standard fern pot with clip-type wire hanger, clay hanging pot, Oriental bowl in a macramé sling.*

More exciting *than standard pottery fare are pots shown below. Some are commercially made; others are handmade. Lower right pot is fashioned from a gourd.*

Foreground: Swedish ivy (*Plectranthus australis*); center: grape ivy (*Cissus rhombifolia*)

Hanging plants indoors

If you like house plants, you'll love them suspended from the ceiling or against a wall. Up in the air, they'll provide a touch of unique, unexpected indoor decor, yet not take up floor space, often at a premium in small apartments.

At plant shops and nurseries, you'll find many house plants suitable for hanging. Boston ferns, for example, can lend a distinguished touch; such loosely flowing types as the spider plant are more casual. Several hanging plants can create a junglelike solarium atmosphere. Or choose flowering species (perhaps a Christmas cactus) for cheerful winter bloom. Indoors is also a good place to display decorative hangers and containers that will accent and complement your plant.

Christmas cactus
(*Schlumbergera bridgesii*)

Wandering Jew (*Zebrina pendula*)

Boston fern (*Nephrolepis exaltata* 'Bostoniense')

Spider plant
(*Chlorophytum comosum*)

21

(Continued from page 19)

into the soil. (Plants growing in plastic containers when you buy them are probably well adapted; you needn't transplant them into more porous containers or worry about their health.)

Very beautiful, though perhaps more expensive and less commonly available than other pots, hand-thrown clay pots, glazed or unglazed, are particularly suited for the drama and showpiece quality of hanging plants. Creations of individual craftsmen and potters, each is unique and often sold along with a specially designed and handmade hanger. You may or may not find hand-thrown pots at a nursery: the best sources usually are handcraft shops, ceramic and pottery stores, and craft fairs.

Choose these pots and your plants carefully together, perhaps selecting a plant with delicate foliage (a small-leafed ivy, such as one of the *Hedera helix* varieties, for example) that will accent, not hide or overwhelm the beauty of the pot.

Because of their fine, decorative designs and glazes, you'll probably want to use handmade pots indoors where they are less apt to be damaged and can be featured as artistic products.

Whether they are glazed or unglazed, clay or plastic, commercially made or created by hand, pots come in a variety of changing styles as new ideas are introduced. Below are descriptions of some of the common pot designs suitable for hanging. Most of them are available in terra cotta, glazed clay, and plastic. By no means should you feel limited only to those described. Undoubtedly you'll run across many others not mentioned that would be fine for hanging. Just keep in mind how your choice will be suspended and how it will appear in the air.

Pots designed for hanging. Sometimes sold as hanging baskets (but not to be confused with wire or plastic baskets, page 23), ceramic, terra cotta, and plastic hanging pots come in shapes ranging from bowls to strawberry jars. Which ones you'll find available depends on the manufacturer who supplies your garden shop.

Most commonly, pots designed for hanging are somewhat bowl shaped, with rounded sides and bottom. Holes in the rim accommodate wire, chain, or rope hangers, or you can suspend them in a sling hanger. On many, the hanger is part of the design. Sizes usually range from 7 to 16 inches in diameter at the rim. Terra cotta versions generally have thicker sides than their earthbound relatives: the extra thickness helps hold in moisture.

Two common variations of the typical bowl-shaped hanging pot are quite popular. One is a strawberry jar with pockets around the sides; holes in its rim facilitate hanging. (A version of this type of jar has one flat side so it can be suspended against a wall.) If you can't find a strawberry jar made for hanging, suspend a small standard jar that has only one or two rows of pockets in a sling hanger. The other variation is a hollow globe with two or three openings in the upper portion for plants. The affair hangs from a single cord or chain attached at the top of the pot.

Some hanging pots have drainage holes but many don't. If you'd like one with a drainage hole, try the plastic kind which includes a drip saucer that clips underneath.

Standard flower and fern pots. Though not specifically designed for hanging, flower and fern pots are the types of containers many people first think of at the mention of "pots." Both have a rim that is thicker than the sides and forms a lip that typifies the design. The sides taper slightly inwards toward the bottom. This basic shape is the same for terra cotta, glazed ceramic, and plastic versions. A wide range of sizes from small to large is available for both fern and flower pots, as are matching drip saucers to catch draining water. (See page 34 for ways to hang pots with drip saucers.) Of the two types of pots, the fern pots are often the most attractive when hung. Also known as three-quarter pots (or azalea pots), these pots are shorter than standard flower pots, which are usually at least as tall as they are wide and often appear out of proportion when filled with some trailing, spreading plants.

You can suspend flower and fern pots from a commercial wire hanger that clips onto the lip of the pot, or you can place the pot in one of the many sling hangers. Try hanging a pot in a wall bracket or placing one on a wooden plant rack.

Oriental pots. Ceramic and terra cotta Oriental pots are shaped like a salad bowl, having straight sides that taper sharply from a wide rim to a narrow base. They are suitable for hanging in slings. Some have holes in the rim for hook-type hangers. They come in sizes ranging from about 8 inches on up to 24 inches. You're better off using small and medium sizes (8 to 12 inches); the larger ones can be heavy and difficult to hang.

Bowls. Quite attractive and easy to hang in slings, bowls have gently curved and rounded sides. Their only drawback is a shallow depth that might not provide enough root room for larger plants. But many low, spreading plants—such as alyssum, African daisy, and gazania—are quite attractive in bowls or planters, especially when planted with a more upright specimen—dwarf marigolds, perhaps—in the center.

Bowls range in size from about 10 to 14 inches across. They sometimes come in deep and shallow versions. Try to get the deeper kind that will provide more room for roots to grow and also be more stable in the air.

Wooden boxes

Attractive and especially appropriate for large perennials and shrubs, wooden boxes come in many styles with holes or hooks in the edge for wire, chain, or rope hangers. Boxes are usually made of redwood or cedar and they mellow nicely with age. Their rustic look and their tendency to drip water, even when lined and not

Wooden boxes *take many forms. Some have holes in the edge for hangers; others have hook or eye screws in the rim.*

Deep wire basket *(left), fine for bouquet plantings; plastic types (right) may not hold plants in sides; shallow wall basket (bottom) takes low plants.*

provided with drainage holes, make them more appropriate in the garden than indoors.

Some boxes are treated with preservative on the inside or have a metal or plastic lining to help hold in moisture and prevent rotting. If yours is lined and proves to have poor drainage, water it as you would an undrained pot (see page 38) or drill drainage holes in its bottom (page 19).

Available box designs may differ from one nursery to another and they may be sold under different names, depending on the manufacturer. Some boxes have four, six, or eight sides that are straight up and down or taper in various degrees out from the bottom. Other boxes are similar in shape to a small barrel and have an opening cut into one side for planting. Another box style, sometimes constructed with spaces between the pieces of wood forming the sides, is reminiscent of a log cabin. (These open-sided boxes must be lined on the inside with moss before planting to keep the soil from spilling out. See page 27 for instructions on lining containers with moss.)

Wooden boxes come in styles that can be mounted on a wall as well as suspended in the air. They usually have a hole in one side for hanging on a strong nail. On others, a loop of cord or rope is attached to one side.

Free-hanging boxes have three or four hooks or holes in the rim to which you can attach a rope, wire, or chain hanger. If you want to use a box that doesn't already have holes or hooks in the rim, add them yourself. (Hooks are available at hardware stores. Use an electric or hand drill to make holes in the box about ½ inch below the rim.)

Baskets

Quite different from pots and boxes, baskets have a character all their own. Really just an open frame, they must be lined on the inside with moss to hold in the soil and plants. In addition to the natural quality of the moss lining, the appeal of baskets lies in the fact that their sides, as well as their top, can be planted to create an entire sphere of foliage or flowers.

Both wire and plastic baskets are available. Wire baskets are most traditional; some gardeners prefer them to plastic types because of their durability, planting ease (you can bend the wire to set plants in the sides), and because the wires become totally enveloped by the moss.

Sizes of both wire and plastic baskets generally range from 8 to 18 inches in diameter. When selecting a size, be sure to allow for about 2 or 3 inches of moss lining around the sides as well as 2 inches of new soil around the plant's roots. A 12 to 14-inch basket should be fine for a plant growing in a 1-gallon can.

Wire and plastic baskets are both quite easy to hang from three or four wires or lengths of chain hooked through the spaces in the rim and joined together at the top. Plastic types may already have a hanger attached when you buy them.

As with wooden boxes, you can get baskets with one flat side designed for hanging against a wall from a nail or picture hanger. A container of this type appears in the right foreground of this book's cover.

Since the moss lining is the only insulation between air and soil, baskets are quite porous and have a tendency to dry out very quickly. They also freely drain water from the sides and bottom. You will probably prefer to limit their use to the garden and avoid hanging them above any surface that stains easily or is difficult to clean.

Baskets come in several shapes: some are deep with fairly straight sides, others are shallow and wider at the rim than they are deep, and some have a rim that rolls inward. In choosing a basket shape, consider the plants you want to grow in it and whether you want to plant the sides as well as the top. Low-growing plants are perhaps best in shallow baskets that will not appear out of proportion or too tall. Deep baskets with straight sides are best suited for large spreading plants whose roots need a lot of room to grow; they are also a good choice if you want to set plants in the sides.

How to plant in containers

If you buy a plant that isn't already growing in a container suitable for hanging, you'll have to put it in one that is. Transplanting is an easy job even if you're new to gardening. Technically, all you do is remove the plant from its container, set it into a new one, and then fill in around the roots with potting soil. Of course, you do all this before hanging the container. Pots and boxes with solid sides are planted in a similar manner. Baskets and boxes with open spaces in the sides require special planting techniques which are described on pages 26-31.

Potting soil

Garden soil is generally too heavy for container plants. Ideal potting soil is loose enough to contain much air and will absorb enough moisture to supply the roots while still allowing excess water to drain from between soil particles.

Commercially mixed potting soil is sterilized to kill pests, diseases, and weeds. Available in sacks of various sizes at most nurseries and garden centers it saves you the trouble of mixing your own. A 2-cubic-foot sack should provide enough soil for you to plant 12 to 15 specimens from gallon cans into 10 or 12-inch containers. Mixes are available for indoor and outdoor plants, as well as for acid-loving plants.

Many gardeners prefer to mix their own potting soil. The ingredients are available at most nurseries, and soil made from them will be free of pests, diseases, and weeds. If you use materials from your garden or some that you've collected at a beach or river, rinse salt and algae from sand, remove any undecomposed stems and leaves from organic matter, and sterilize the final mixture by baking it in shallow pans in the oven for 2 hours at 180°. (The terrible smell of baking soil won't last long.)

If you don't have a favorite recipe for potting soil, here's a good basic mix that's fine for most outdoor plants: 16 gallons (about 2 cubic feet) of nitrogen-stabilized bark, redwood sawdust, peat moss, or other organic matter; 8 gallons (about 1 cubic foot) of sandy loam or uniform fine sand; 1⅓ cups of 0-10-10 or equivalent dry fertilizer; and 1¾ cups of dolomite limestone. Mixed in the given amounts, the recipe will provide about 3 cubic feet of soil.

Azaleas and other plants in the Ericaceae family need a soil that's slightly more acid than the basic mix. Blend together 4 or 5 parts of coarse-textured peat moss and one part composted leaf mold.

Indoor and shade-loving plants should be grown in a soil that's lighter than the basic mix; combine 1 part perlite with 2 parts of the basic soil.

A wheel barrow or a clean swept concrete driveway will serve as a good mixing place. Be sure to blend all soil ingredients thoroughly, eliminate any stones, and break up large lumps. Store leftover soil in a clean trash can or a large plastic sack. Keep the soil dry.

Planting in pots and boxes

Before planting in a used pot or box, clean it well with hot water and a brush, especially if it might be the home of pests and diseases from previous plants and soil. Porous containers should be soaked in water so that, when planted, they won't absorb moisture from the soil.

Preparing to plant. If your container has a drainage hole in the bottom, place a curved piece of broken pottery or a section of fine-mesh wire screen over it to prevent clogging and to minimize soil filtering through.

In an undrained container, add about a ½ to 1-inch layer of coarse sand and then an equal layer of granulated charcoal to the bottom to lessen soil souring. The charcoal used in containers is available in sacks at nurseries and garden centers. Do not use barbecue charcoal.

After covering the drain hole or adding the sand and charcoal to the bottom of the container, pour in some moist, but not soaking wet, potting soil. This soil cushion should be deep enough so that, when you set in the plant, the surface of its root ball will be about one or two inches below the rim of the container.

Setting in the plant. Remove your plant from its container; then set it on the cushion of soil in the new one. To take a plant out of a small pot, turn it upside down with one hand and gently shake and rap it to loosen the root ball while supporting the top of the root ball with the other hand. If your plant is in a 1-gallon can, use tin snips to cut the sides apart (the nurseryman can do this for you); then lift out the plant. (Be careful of the sheared edges of the can, for they can give you a nasty cut.) Bedding plants growing in flats can be individually removed—as you do brownies from a pan—with a spatula or putty knife; don't use a trowel. Leave a little soil around the roots of each plant. Bedding plants can be removed from plastic cell packs by pushing up from the bottom.

To plant in a box or pot, *first set broken pottery over drain hole (if the container is undrained, add a layer of sand and charcoal).* **Left:** *Pour in some moist potting mix.* **Above:** *Set plants into container on soil layer. Plants can be closer together in containers than in the ground.*

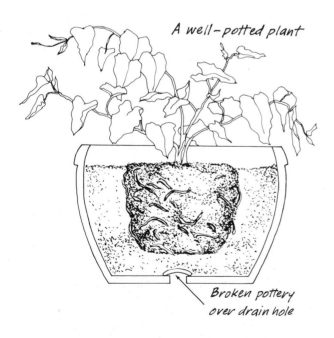

A well-potted plant

Broken pottery over drain hole

With plants in the container, *add soil around their roots, tamping it down with your fingers.*

Well-potted plant *has an inch or two of new soil around root ball, sits an inch or so below rim of container. Crockery over drain hole keeps in soil.*

Finally, water *the planted container thoroughly and let the plants rest in a protected location for a day or so before hanging them up.*

Planting (cont'd.)

If you notice that the roots of the plant show through or are tightly compacted around the outside of the root ball, lightly score them in several places with a sharp knife and loosen them gently with your fingers so they'll begin to grow outward in the new container rather than continue to twine around themselves.

Place the plant in the new container so the top of its root ball is about 1 or 2 inches below the rim. Plants can be set closer together in containers than in the garden.

Fill in around the container's sides and between the plants with moist potting mix. Raise the soil level around the plants about 2 or 3 inches at a time, tamping down each layer of soil lightly with your fingers or a stick to settle it in firmly. Continue filling and tamping the sides until they are level with the surface of the plant's root ball.

Post-planting care. After potting the plant, water it carefully until excess water begins to run out the drainage hole. If your pot or box is undrained, apply an amount of water equal to about one-quarter of the total volume of the soil in the container. (See pages 38-39 for more watering details.)

Before permanently hanging the newly potted plant, set it in a shady, protected location for a day or two where it will receive mild, even temperatures and can recuperate from the shock of transplanting. Plants need time to adjust to a new home just as you do.

Planting in baskets

Looking at an empty wire basket, you may well wonder how in the world its open sides will hold in your plant and soil. Indeed, planting in a basket differs from putting plants in solid-sided boxes and pots, but only in two ways: you must line the inside of the basket with moss before planting, and, if you wish, you can set plants in the sides of the basket as well as on the top. (Wooden boxes with open sides are lined with moss just as baskets are, but the spaces may not be large enough for setting plants in the sides.)

Choose a basket that will leave about 2 or 3 inches for new soil around the plant's roots and also 2 or 3 inches all around for the moss lining. Most plants growing in a 1-gallon can or a 6-inch pot will fit nicely into a 12 or 14-inch basket. Use a 14 or 16-inch size for two 1-gallon can plants. A 14 or 16-inch basket is also recommended for bouquet plantings.

Moss. When you purchase your basket, buy some moss with which to line it. Moss comes either commercially packaged in plastic sacks or in handfuls that the nurseryman just loads into a bag or into your empty basket. It will come in irregular sheets or clumps. Either sheets or clumps will be fine, though with experience you may develop a preference.

Be sure to get enough moss to fully line your basket with a 2 or 3-inch layer that extends about 2 inches

Small annual plants *often come in plastic cell packs. Remove plant by pushing up from bottom of cell.*

If roots of a plant *show through or twine around outside of root ball, gently loosen them.*

You make these hanging planters

Hand tools and weathered wood are all you need to make these three simple wooden planters. The rustic shapes can be built from scrap redwood or perhaps recycled wood from an old building. Snoop around the back of a lumber yard for pieces that have been left out long enough to mellow.

The hexagonal planter uses 2-inch number 10 screws to attach the 1-inch-thick sides to the 2-inch-thick ends. Counter sink and then fill over screws with wood plugs or wood putty. The other two boxes are held together with 8-penny finishing nails (also counter sunk and filled over with wood putty). In all of the planters, the pieces are bonded with waterproof resorcinol glue.

After the planters are assembled and the glue is dry, round the edges with a wood rasp or open-toothed shaper. Drill drain holes as needed. Drill holes in the edges (or apply screw hooks or screw eyes) to accommodate a wire, chain, or rope hanger.

Since the idea is to arrive at a hand-hewn look, no sanding or finishing (other than rounding the edges) is necessary. Oil might be used to darken and help preserve the wood.

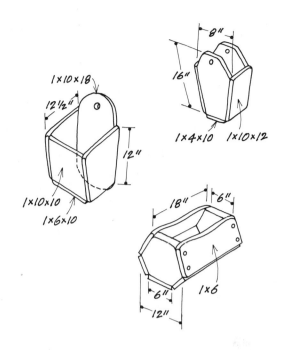

above the rim. A 240-cubic-inch bag (or about three or four good-sized handfuls) should be plenty for a 12-inch basket.

Lining the basket with moss. Start your basket by lining the inside with moss. (See top photos, page 30.) Moss is easiest to work with when damp. Thoroughly soak it for 15 or 20 minutes in a basin or tubful of clean water. (Moss may be somewhat water repellent at first.) When it's completely soaked, gently squeeze and shake out excess water and let the moss drain for 15 or 20 minutes.

Apply the damp moss to the inside of the basket to create a 2 or 3-inch-thick lining along the sides and bottom that extends about 2 inches above the basket's rim. If the moss is in sheet form, lay sections of it up and down the sides, cutting to fit as necessary. Overlap adjacent sections. With clumps of moss, use large, matted pieces, tucking the upper edge of each clump around a convenient frame member of the basket to hold the clump in place. Fit each piece of moss so that it overlaps neighboring pieces like shingles on a roof. Be certain to fill in any thin or open spaces in the lining. Before continuing with the planting, let the moss lining dry out slightly until it's firmed into place.

While lining the basket, you will probably experience one vexation: it will tend to roll onto its sides. This can be especially difficult when you begin planting. To hold a basket upright, set its bottom in a terra cotta pot or any other stable container; or you can temporarily hang the basket at an easy height for planting from an overhead nail or hook. Be sure the basket is securely, though temporarily, hung when you plant because its weight will quickly increase as soil and plants are added.

Setting in the plants. The process of planting a basket is slightly different if you plant only the top or both the top and the sides. Let's look first at the routine for planting the top alone.

Knock your plant from its present container as described for planting in pots and boxes. Then fill your basket with moist potting soil (page 24) until the top of the plant's root ball will be 1 or 2 inches below the basket's rim (not the top of the moss lining) when you set it into the basket.

Now place the plant on the soil cushion and fill in around the sides with potting mix to level them up with the top of the root ball. Firm the soil down as you add it to the sides but don't compress it tightly.

Securely hang the finished basket in a protected area to rest for a day or two, watering it gently and thoroughly. Continue watering even after excess water begins draining out the bottom and sides. Dry moss is somewhat water repellent, but, once it does become damp, it will absorb water from the soil.

To plant the sides of a wire basket as well as the top—a technique frequently used with small flowering plants to create a sphere of color—follow the instructions and photographs on pages 30-31.

English ivy
(*Hedera helix*)

Pelargonium (*P. peltatum* 'Mrs. Banks')

Peperomia
(*P. griseo-argentea*)

Containers and hangers: half the picture

It's often a toss-up as to whether the plant or the container and hanger has the most appeal in airborne arrangements. In one unique arrangement, several containers are suspended one above the other. The tiered example below was commercially made; other types may be of macramé or rope. (See page 34 for other tiered hangers.)

Many containers and hangers are handmade and have graceful form or elaborate finishes. Others incorporate polished wood. To best show them off, select plants with delicate foliage or semi-upright growth, such as an ivy or 'Fluffy Ruffles' fern.

For something really extraordinary, try planting in such objects as the hollowed-out crevice of a gnarled piece of driftwood, a spaghetti strainer, or even an old shoe.

'Fluffy Ruffles' fern
(*Nephrolepis exaltata* 'Fluffy Ruffles')

Petunias, sweet alyssum,
marigolds

29

1 and 2. *Begin to plant your basket by lining it with damp moss. Work up the sides, using sheets or clumps of moss. Overlap each piece to prevent holes. The finished lining should be about 2 inches thick and extend about 2 inches above basket rim. Fill holes, thin spots with small moss pieces.*

6 and 7. *Continue planting around basket to complete first level. Set plants close together (2 or 3 inches apart). Use different plants to create patterns of color. When first level is planted (with root balls resting on soil in basket), rebend wires, repair lining around stems with bits of moss, and tamp soil around roots to bring soil up to next planting level.*

8. *Continue planting each successive level as you did the first. Be sure to repair the moss lining around the plants' stems with bits of moss.*

Planting in baskets... how to make a living bouquet

3. After lining the basket, pour in a layer of potting soil up to the first level you want to plant.

4. With your fingers or a sharp knife, make small openings or slits (one for each plant) in the moss lining between the basket's wires just above soil level.

5. Gently push each plant's root ball through a hole or slit in moss. Bend wires or loosen root ball (page 26) if it won't easily fit through the wires.

9 and 10. Stop planting basket sides about 6 inches from rim; fill soil around roots of last level; set plants in top of basket as you would in a pot or box; fill in with soil.

Getting It Off the Ground

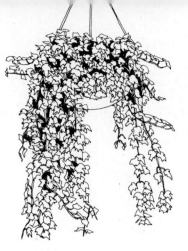

Hanging a plant is as much a matter of common sense as it is of technical know-how and high-wire artistry. Basically, all you do is attach a hanger to your container, lift it up, and hook the end of the hanger to the overhead support you have chosen. This support might be a ceiling, beam, roof overhang, patio structure, tree limb, or a wall—anything that is strong enough to bear the weight of your container. (See pages 6-16 for ideas on where to locate your plant and what to look for in an overhead support.)

Most hangers have a hook, ring, or loop at the top. It is easiest and safest to hang them from a hook or eye that's been screwed into the structure above. Using a nail instead may seem the quickest solution, but nails can bend, pull loose, or the container can slip off them.

When hanging a container from a tree limb, use a hook rather than a length of wire, chain, or rope around a branch. Wire, chain, or rope can damage the tree, even if it's padded with garden hose, heavy cloth, or other material.

Have a friend help you hang your plant and use a ladder or chair rather than trying to reach too high. Release the container slowly to make sure the hanger, hook, and overhead structure are all secure and not about to break or pull loose.

Hangers for containers

Some containers come complete with the hanger as part of the package. If you choose a type without a hanger, you'll have to buy or make one.

Almost all hanger designs fall into two basic types: rim or sling.

• Rim hangers generally consist of three or four strands of material which are joined at the top and which hook or clip onto the edge of a container. Though rim hangers are usually made of wire, chain, plastic, or rope, they may also be of macramé or braided strands.

• Sling hangers, unlike rim hangers, do not attach on the edge of the container but instead go under and around the container, cradling it in a hammocklike fashion. Sling hangers most often are made of macramé or leather but, like rim hangers, can be fashioned from rope, chain, or other materials.

In addition to rim and sling hangers, you may come across suspended wooden frames and wall brackets in which a container sits. Sometimes a platform on which a pot is placed serves as a hanger. Some hangers can be adapted to include a drip saucer.

When selecting a plant hanger, make sure it will fit your container. Rim-type chain, wire, or rope hangers usually require a container that has holes, hooks, or eye screws in its edge. Most containers designed specifically for hanging have these provisions; on baskets you just bend or hook the strands through openings in the frame. But be sure to get a three or four-strand rim hanger to match the three or four holes or hooks in your container.

Drilling your own holes in the edge of a pot may be possible, but it can be tricky. On a clay pot, use a carbide bit in an electric drill and set the pot over the corner of a wooden bench or sawhorse for support. Use a standard bit in an electric drill to make holes in a plastic pot or wooden box. As an alternative to drilling, apply three or four hooks in the edge of the box.

Because sling hangers can be used on pots with or without holes, they make fine supports for ground containers not specifically designed for the air. Be sure your container will fit into the sling you plan to use. While commercially made wire and chain rim-type hangers will fit most containers up to about 16 inches in diameter (design your own hanger if the container is larger), slings aren't always uniform in design and may only fit a narrow range of container sizes.

Some slings form a network that extends well above the container's rim. Although these are suitable for containers holding small plants that aren't fully drooping, they can restrict the growth of plants that do spill over a container's edge.

When setting a planted container into a sling, be careful that the stems and foliage don't become pinched between the hanger and the container's sides.

You can use both the sling and rim-type hangers with drained or undrained containers and with or without a drip saucer beneath the drained containers. Since dripping water can damage some hangers, especially those made of macramé, leather, or other decorative material, seriously consider placing a drip saucer beneath a drained container in a sling. Sling hangers are not suitable for baskets because of the moss sides.

In choosing a hanger, consider how high off the ground you want the plant suspended. Lowering a hanging plant is relatively easy with most hangers, but raising it more than a few inches may be difficult.

Wire hangers

Commercially made wire hangers, available at nurseries and garden centers, usually have three or four 24-inch-length strands of 12 or 14-gauge single strand galvanized wire. At one end the strands are joined and bent or attached to a hook or loop. The other end of each strand is bent through a hole or hook in the rim of a pot or box or through the spaces between the frame of a basket. One type of wire hanger is a two-strand hanger that clips onto the rim of flower and fern pots. (These clip-on hangers may tend to slip off glazed pots.)

A feature of some, but not all, wire hangers is a swivel at the joint between the strands and the hook. The swivel permits you to rotate the container easily for balanced light exposure on all sides of the plant. (Grip the hook to hold it steady while you turn the container.)

When setting up a wire hanger, watch that the weight of the container doesn't pull the wires out of the container holes. Secure the strands to the container by bending them through the holes or hooks in the container's edge and then twisting them into loops.

You can adjust the height of a wire-hung container, raising it by bending lengths of each strand through the edge of the container or lowering it by attaching the hook at the top to a single overhead extension wire or chain.

Chain hangers

Basically similar to wire hangers, chain hangers consist of three or four lengths joined at one end to a hook or ring and attached to hooks or holes in the container's rim at the other end.

Chain hangers are inexpensive and easy to make. All the materials are available at a good hardware store. Get three or four (depending on the number of hooks or holes in your container) equal lengths of chain, an S hook to join the lengths at the top, and perhaps three or four more S hooks to attach them to your container.

Chain comes in many styles and sizes and is made of galvanized or brass-plated iron or steel, solid brass, or even colored plastic. Twisted lengths of some chains have a decorative appeal.

Three or four-strand hangers made of chain about a number 16 or 14 in size (the larger the number, the smaller the chain) should be strong enough to hold most average-size containers.

The lengths of chain should be just a few inches longer than the level you want the container to hang. If your overhead support is very high, it might be easier and less expensive to buy short lengths just 2 feet long and then connect them at the top to a single length of heavier chain that you can easily shorten or lengthen to adjust the final height of the container.

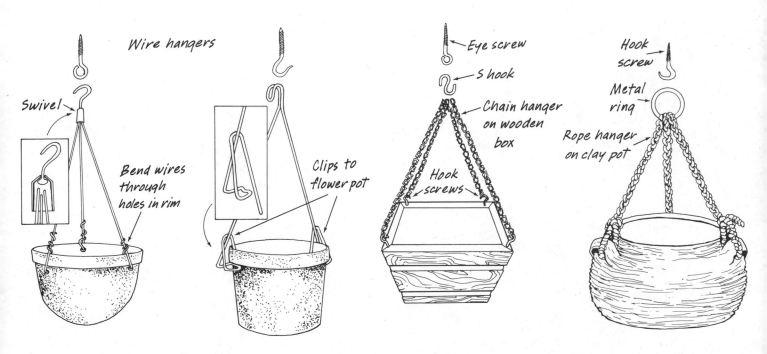

Two commercial wire hangers. *If yours doesn't have a built-in swivel, use a fishing line swivel.*

Chain and rope hangers. *Chain hangers are easily put together. Hooks let you hang standard boxes.*

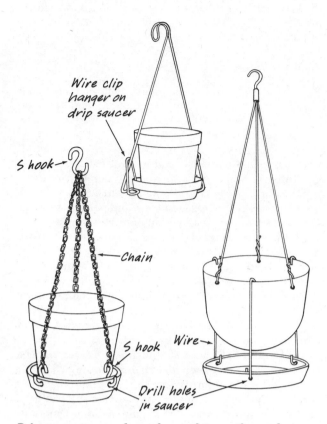

Drip saucers *can hang beneath pots from chain or wire. Use carbide bit to drill necessary holes.*

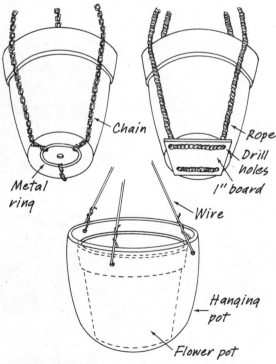

Homemade sling-type hangers *utilize metal ring or square of wood. Or set standard pot in hanging pot.*

Hangers (cont'd.)

Rope and plastic hangers

A good, flexible material for a hanger, rope often has a pleasing, rustic character. You can rig a rope suspender to the rim of a container by tying three or four equal lengths together at one end and knotting the other end of each through holes or hooks in the container's edge.

Most of the different kinds of rope available at a hardware store—nylon, hemp, or cotton in woven or twisted strands—will hold your container. Check the test weight of the rope you choose to make sure it's strong enough for your container.

Try monofilament clear-plastic fishing line sold in sporting goods stores as a sling hanger. The effect is quite unique: the plant appears to float unsupported in the air. To make a plastic line sling hanger, use a square of clear plastic or thin plywood as a base for the container to sit on. Drill four holes in it for two lengths of line to pass through as they go beneath the container.

Macramé, leather, woven, and braided hangers

If you're looking for an unusual and decorative hanger, try one in macramé or leather or one that's braided or woven. Often already attached to an attractive container, they're sold in nurseries and plant shops; but you might also find one in a handcraft shop, import store, patio shop, or at a craft fair.

Usually handmade, these hangers come in innumerable designs: some are attached to the rim of the container; others form a sling, and some hold two or

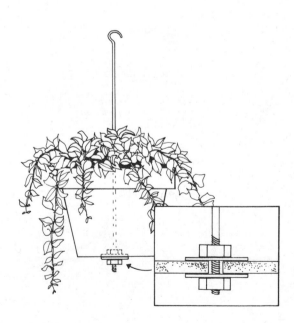

Threaded metal rod *can be bolted through drain hole in flower or fern pot to get it off the ground.*

more pots, one above the other piggyback style.

When you buy a handmade hanger, make sure it fits your container and is strong enough to take the load. The best macramé, braided, and woven hangers are made of strong cord or twine. If the one you choose is made of yarn, use it only with a small container that won't unduly stretch or break it. Check for stretching as knots tighten.

These types of hangers are often best suited to the indoors, where they won't be exposed to damaging weather; they may appear out of place if used with wire baskets and wooden boxes. Watch for rotting on older rope, macramé, and leather hangers, especially if they've been used outdoors.

To make your own decorative hanger, follow instructions on macramé, leatherwork, and braiding in an appropriate craft book.

Plant racks

Rather than hang the container itself, why not suspend a plant rack on which you can put one, two, or more containers? Plant racks are generally made of wood and are convenient because they attractively support such common but hard-to-hang containers as standard flower and fern pots.

You may find various designs of plant racks in nurseries, plant shops, import stores, and craft shops and fairs. You can also make a plant rack at home. In a 1-inch-thick board, use a key hole or saber saw to cut a hole for each container you want to hang. The holes should be an inch or two smaller than the greatest diameter of the container. Now drill a hole or place a hook or eye screw in each corner of the board for a wire, rope, or chain hanger. You can also make a square or triangular frame (use 1 by 2s or similar lumber) slightly smaller than the width of the container.

Rigid hangers

A wooden box can be held aloft by two 2 by 4s (or 1 by 1s if the box is small and light) firmly bolted to opposite sides and bolted with L-brackets to an overhead beam, overhang, or eve.

Many pots with drainage holes can be hung by bolting the threaded end of a metal rod through the hole. There should be a bolt and washer on the part of the rod just inside the container and another bolt and washer on the outside of the pot. Tighten the outside bolt until the pot is secured tightly between the two washers. Then set the plant in the container, working its roots around the vertical rod. (See page 34).

Fashion a macramé hanger

Equipment and materials: scissors, one 18 inch by 18 inch square of ceiling tile, T-pins, ruler, pencil, eight 4-yard lengths (folded in half) of 27-thread white cotton cable cord, one 2-inch diameter brass ring, four ceramic dangles or large-holed beads.
1. Attach folded cords to the brass ring at folds as shown in the top drawing. Then group the cords into four groups of 4 working strands each. Tape the ring to the center of the tile board.
2. Using the two center cords of each group of four as holding cords, tie one square knot with the two outside cords of each group (see drawing).
3. Make a second row of square knots, placing them 1½ inches away from and in between the first square knots (see drawing).
4. Make three more alternating rows of square knots, increasing the distance between the new knots and the previous row of knots by ½ inch each time a new row is begun. When the last row of knots is finished, use the two center cords of each knot to tie on the ceramic dangles or beads.
5. After the bead is knotted on, use each group of four strands to make four chains of 14 or more square knots. With the chains completed, twist 7 of the 8 strands together; then double them over into a loop. Wrap the eighth strand around and up the loop, securing it by separating it into three twists and knotting it around the loop. Trim off any loose ends as needed.

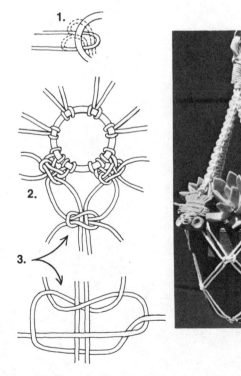

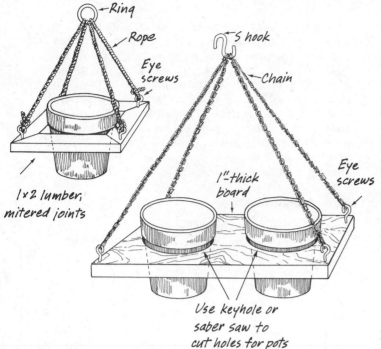

Flower or fern pots *sit in homemade wooden plant racks; lip of pots prevents their falling through.*

Wall mounts and brackets

If you lack a convenient overhead support from which to hang a plant, you can always put it up in the air against a wall or post. Wall baskets are generally half round and hang from a hook, bolt, or nail in a wall. Boxes designed for wall hanging usually have a hole in one side for a bolt or are rigged like a picture frame with a rope or wire loop.

Pots, especially standard flower and fern pots, can be set in wall brackets that hang against a wall. Often wrought iron or wood, the brackets have one, two, or three round hoops for the pots to sit in. One type of wall mount is a small metal bracket that clips onto the rim of a small flower or fern pot. A sheet of plastic placed between the container and the wall can help prevent wall stains.

Using hooks and other hardware

Most hangers are easiest to suspend if there is a hook or eye in the overhead support. (Some can just be looped around an open beam.) Hook and eye screws are available in a range of sizes at hardware stores and in the household section of many supermarkets. A number 4, 6, or 8 size should be sufficient for most containers. (Sizes increase as the numbers become smaller.) A size 10 or even smaller might be enough to hold a light container. Use a number 2, 1, 0, or 00 for very large and heavy containers.

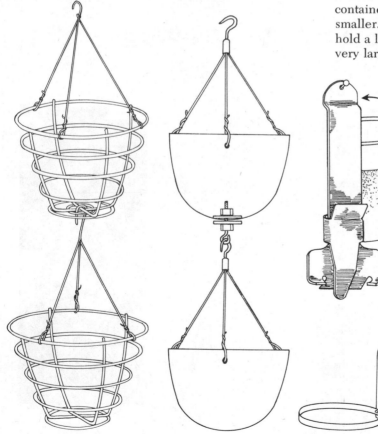

For tiered hangers, *use small baskets or pots that won't break from the weight and strain.*

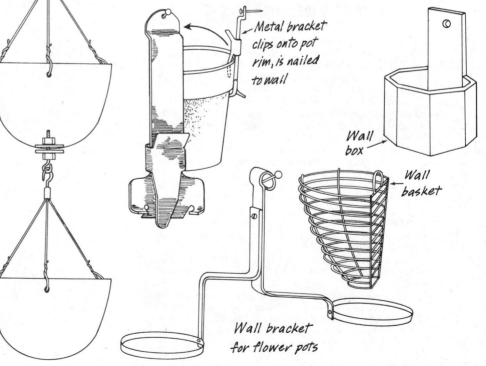

Wooden boxes, baskets *come in wall-mounting styles. Wall brackets, clip device hold flower pots.*

Cup hooks have a somewhat more finished appearance than standard iron or steel types and look well indoors; use them for light containers. You might also try safety hooks that have a flexible strip of metal closing over the opening in the hook to prevent the hanger from slipping.

If your hanger has a ring or loop in the end, select a hook screw or buy an S hook (they're shaped like the letter S) that will adapt it to an eye screw. An eye screw is most appropriate for hangers with a hook on the end, but you can also use a hook screw if you're sure the hanger won't slip off it. If your hanger doesn't have a swivel at the top, you can use a fishing line swivel: get a large one, such as a number 1 standard type or a ball bearing type designed for deep sea fishing.

Hook or eye screws with a pointed end will screw directly into most wooden structures that are thick and sturdy enough to give their threads a secure grip. To facilitate the job of applying them, you can drill a pilot hole.

Not all the structures you might want to hang your plant from will be wooden. The ceilings and walls of many homes are gypsum board or plaster over lath, attached to a framework of ceiling joists (usually wooden 2 by 6s or 2 by 8s) or wall studs (generally 2 by 4s) spaced 16 inches apart. (On some buildings they may be 20 or 24 inches apart.) The gypsum board or plaster alone won't usually offer the resiliency to hold the threads of a screw. You should locate a ceiling joist or wall stud, drill a pilot hole, and screw in a hook or eye whose threaded end is long enough to penetrate the stud or joist. (To locate ceiling joists and wall studs, see page 14.)

If it isn't convenient for you to find a joist or stud where you want the plant to hang, you might use a fiber sleeve, an expansion bolt, or a toggle bolt to secure your hook or eye to the ceiling or wall. Be careful when using these devices, especially fiber sleeves, for they may not be strong enough to bear the direct downward pull of even medium-sized (9-inch) containers.

A fiber sleeve is inserted into a hole drilled into the ceiling or wall. When you screw a hook or eye into it (sleeves have a hole in the center), the sleeve expands to tightly grip the sides of the hole. Expansion bolts are screwed or inserted into a drilled hole; when a hook or eye is tightened into them, they mushroom out, gripping the inside of the wall. (Most expansion bolts come with a standard machine bolt that you will want to replace with an eye or hook bolt having machine-type threads.) Toggle bolts are screwed onto the end of a hook or eye bolt and then inserted through a drilled hole; they expand to grip the inside of the wall. (A washer between the outside of the wall and the eye or hook will hide the hole.)

You might hesitate before using expansion bolts and toggle bolts since they require a somewhat large hole that may be difficult to fill. Expansion bolts are also nonremovable—you must set them slightly below the surface of the wall before they can be covered over.

Use lead anchors (they are similar to fiber sleeves) to secure hook and eye screws to brick, concrete, and masonry. Drill a hole in the structure that's the same diameter as the anchor and slightly deeper than its length. Use either a carbide bit in an electric drill or a hammer and a star drill to make the hole. When you insert the anchor and screw in the hook or eye, the anchor will expand to create a tight fit.

Hooks and eyes can create holes in a wall or ceiling that the manager or owner of your rented apartment might not appreciate. To fill a hole, use wood filler or spackling putty, available at hardware stores. Follow the manufacturer's directions for applying both. If necessary, a spot of touch-up paint can camouflage the repair work.

Adjusting height

Desirable heights for hanging plants vary. For watering ease you might want the container low enough that you can see the soil. Spreading plants might be most attractive slightly lower than eye level so you can enjoy their form; long trailing plants can be higher.

If your airborne plant hangs higher or lower than you'd like, there are techniques of adjusting it. The easiest way to lower most containers is to add a single length of wire, chain, rope, or other material to the top of the hanger. Cut a piece of the material the length you want the container lowered. Add an S hook or ring to its ends or tie or twist them into loops or hooks.

Raising a container can be more difficult than lowering it; sometimes it's impossible. If the hanger is attached to the rim of the container, you may be able to take up lengths at the ends of the strands where they go through holes or hooks in the container edge. Another method is to gather together the ends of the strands at the top of the container so they join at a lower point. Both of these methods work only until the junction of the strands begins to press against the plant.

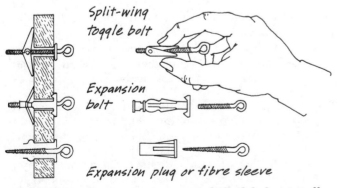

Split-wing toggle bolt

Expansion bolt

Expansion plug or fibre sleeve

Fasteners above *require a pre-drilled hole in wall or ceiling. Use them with light containers.*

Keeping Your Plants Healthy

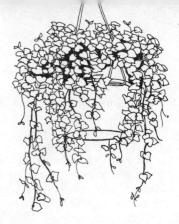

Once it's off the ground, relax and enjoy your hanging plant—but don't neglect it. For strong, healthy growth, airborne plants need basically the same care as container plants on the ground. The degree and kind of care you give depends on the plant. Most plants need water, fertilizer, and regular turning for equal light exposure on all sides. Pinching, training, and special treatment during the winter months may also be required. And don't be surprised if you find yourself at odds with pests and diseases.

Let's see what you can do from the beginning to assure success with your plant.

Culture—the key to a happy plant

Light, sun, temperature, and humidity—all these environmental elements affect the growth of a plant. Since different plants require different growing conditions, providing these conditions will make it far happier than almost anything else—including soothing talk and soft music. After all, trying to grow a sun-loving plant in a dark corner of the house is like trying to raise tropical fish in the bathtub—a dubious if not impossible venture.

If you have a specific plant you want to grow, study its cultural requirements on pages 44-78 and then find a location that meets its needs. If you don't have a particular plant in mind, look around your house or garden and find a location where you'd like a touch of vegetation. After studying the location for a day or two to determine how much sun and shade it gets, choose your plant accordingly.

Tips on locating plants, both in the garden and in the house, and points to consider regarding exposure to sun, shade, light, and heat are given on pages 6-17. You'll also find lists of plants that do well in full sun, shade, part sun/part shade, and indoors in chapter 1.

Watering and feeding

Because all plants need some water and fertilizer, providing them will probably be your most time-consuming responsibility. Actually watering and fertilizing is quite easy; where most gardeners, especially beginners, seem to have trouble is deciding how much and how often to water and feed a plant. The discussion below should help you get started.

Watering

To give your hanging plant a drink, reach up with a hose, watering can, or cup and pour water onto the soil beneath the plant's foliage. Some gardeners find it easiest to take the plant down while watering. (Set it on an inverted pot to protect stems.)

Do a thorough job of watering. To a drained container, apply water until the excess runs freely from the drainage hole for a full minute or longer. Dry soil may not absorb water immediately. Instead, the water may rush quickly through between soil particles. If the soil is dry, don't stop watering until you're sure it has had a chance to take in as much moisture as it can hold.

To a container without a drainage hole, apply a volume of water equal to about one-quarter the total volume of the soil. You'll want to provide enough water for the plant's needs, yet not so much that excess accumulates in the bottom of the container and drowns the plant.

When to water. How frequently you water will depend on the kind of plant you have. Different plants need different amounts of water: many ferns and annuals, for example, like the soil evenly moist all the time; some succulents, on the other hand, resent constantly damp soil.

Generally, plants in hanging containers will need more frequent watering than their counterparts in containers on the ground since they're exposed on all sides—even on the bottom—to drying air.

A rule of thumb is to water as soon as the top inch of soil feels dry when you wiggle your finger in it. There are exceptions to this rule, however, so be sure to read the information on your particular plant (see pages 44-78).

Once you become familiar with your plant, you'll probably develop a watering schedule for it. But don't let a routine prevent you from making between-watering checks on the plant. In a single afternoon, especially hot or windy weather can dry out a container, particularly a basket or other porous type. Similarly, don't assume you can skip your watering just because it has rained. The overhead structure your plant hangs from may shelter it from the benefits of a free shower.

Be careful not to let the moss lining of baskets dry out entirely. When dry, moss is somewhat water repellent. But once it begins taking in moisture, it's like a sponge and will absorb water out of the soil after you've stopped watering.

Just as changes in the weather may alter your day-to-day watering schedule, so may seasonal changes affect your plant's need for water. During the dormant season (usually in the winter or just after a period of heavy bloom), for example, many plants require less water than they do during the active growing season.

Drip. When watering your drained container or basket, you'll probably discover one of the major drawbacks of hanging plants: drip. Solutions to the drip problem are to use an undrained container, suspend a saucer beneath the container, or take your plant down when you water.

Feeding

Plants get most of the nutrients they need from the soil through their roots. As nutrients are used up by a plant or are leached out of the soil by draining water, they must be replenished.

As with watering, it's difficult to prescribe the kind and quantity of fertilizer for a plant and how often you should apply it. You must consider the specific needs of your plant, how frequently you water (draining water leaches out nutrients), and the season (some plants don't need as much food during the dormant season as they do during the period of active growth).

In general, plants in hanging containers benefit from lighter, more frequent feedings than you'd give plants in the garden. This assures a constant source of nutrients for continuous, even growth and minimizes the chance of fertilizer burn or other damage caused by heavy, infrequent fertilizing. Light applications about twice a month should suffice for most plants. One type of fertilizer takes the form of slow release granules that are scratched into the soil surface or mixed into the soil before potting. They dissolve slowly as you water, feeding the plant without your having to make monthly or bimonthly applications.

Fertilizers are composed of three main ingredients. *Nitrogen* encourages foliage growth and helps leaves maintain good color. *Phosphorus* helps the plant build a sturdy root system and promotes flower production. *Potassium* (potash) aids such plant processes as photosynthesis. The ratio of these elements in a given fertilizer is indicated by numbers, such as 5-10-5 or 1-10-10. Foliage plants generally like a high nitrogen fertilizer, such as 30-10-10. Flowering plants benefit from fertilizers high in phosphorus, 15-30-15 for example. Some plants, such as azaleas and camellias, require different formulations, and special fertilizers are available for them. Such complete fertilizers as fish emulsion are fine for most plants.

Just because a little fertilizer is good for a plant, don't assume that more is even better. Excessive feeding, usually indicated by the leaves turning brown and crisp around the edges, can kill a plant. Never fertilize a thirsty plant, even with a light dosage. The plant's roots, anxious for a drink, will suddenly absorb more food in solution with the water than is good for them. Before fertilizing, thoroughly water the plant, giving it about a day to take in the water.

High-hanging containers *outdoors might be watered with an aluminum extension on your garden hose.*

Sometimes it's easiest *to take a plant down for watering. Set it on inverted pot to protect long stems.*

Turning, pinching, training, and off-season care

If you hang garlic in your kitchen, you can forget about it until you're ready to use it. But if you hang plants in your gardens or home, they'll need frequent attention. You should be prepared to turn your plants regularly, pinch them back, train them, and perhaps provide off-season care.

Turning a plant

While your plant is hanging, turn it frequently so all sides will be exposed to an equal amount of light and will grow at the same rate. It's especially important to turn plants in corners, close to windows, or near walls—wherever one side would be exposed to more light than the other. If not turned, plants in locations such as these will show strong vigorous growth on one side and weak spindly growth on the other. Giving the container a quarter or half turn every week should assure even light exposure on all sides.

Some hangers have a swivel at the top that facilitates easy turning. If yours doesn't just reach up and rehang the container on the hook. Or attach a large fishing line swivel between the top of the hanger and the hook or eye screw.

Pinching a plant

A branching plant capable of forming new growing tips along its stems is often "pinched" at the tip of each stem to direct growth into side branches that will create a fuller, bushier display.

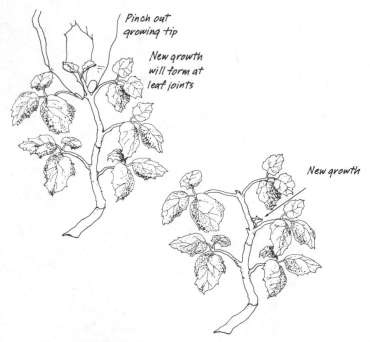

Pinch out growing tip

New growth will form at leaf joints

New growth

To stimulate bushiness, *nip off growing tip of stem. New growth will form at leaf and stem joints.*

To pinch a plant, nip off the growing tip at the end of each stem. Use your fingernails, a sharp knife, or a pair of clippers to make a clean cut just above a set of leaves. In a few weeks or a month, new branches should begin to form along the stem, usually making their first appearance as small pairs of leaves at the joints between established leaves and the stem.

On a plant grown for its foliage, pinch the ends of all but the shortest stems at the beginning of the active growing season when new growth starts to appear at the tips of branches. Continue pinching throughout the season, as necessary, to shape and fill out the plant. But, before pinching a second or third time, be sure to give new side branches a chance to form and establish themselves.

You can pinch a flowering plant until buds begin to form or until the plant is as bushy as you want it. Be sure, though, to stop pinching in time for the plant to bloom before the end of the warm season.

During the blooming season, remove dead and fading blossoms to stimulate the growth of new buds and to maintain general tidiness. To keep growth directed in the leaves and stems, pinch off insignificant flowers on plants grown for their foliage.

Special plant training

A number of container plants and plants whose branches are long and flexible but not necessarily trailing make unique, unexpected hangers when specially trained to droop. (Cutting-grown podocarpus is an example of a home-trained trailer.) You can also train a plant whose stems don't seem to want to dangle as much as you'd like them to.

One method of training a plant is to attach weights to the young branches before they become stiff or woody. You can tie weights—fishing sinkers or washers will work—onto the branches with string or thread. Be careful not to break or overstrain branches; train them in stages if they are too stiff to pull downward all at once. Just apply heavier weights every few weeks.

Off-season plant care

Most plants, even indoor specimens, have a season of at least a month or two of full or semi-dormancy (usually during the winter or just after a period of heavy bloom) when their active growth slows or even stops. During this dormant time, some plants may drop many or all of their leaves; some may even die back to the ground leaving only the roots beneath the soil alive. Other plants may keep all of their leaves but not produce any new growth. Annuals, of course, die entirely once their blooming season is over.

During their inactive period, you may want to take one of several steps to hold perennial plants over until the following season. Some gardeners, especially those in cold-winter climates, find it easiest just to throw out their plants and buy new ones in the spring. Or in the

Insulated wire *weights stems down so they'll trail. Even natural droopers may need training.*

Plectranthus *usually grows full and trails easily, but this one might benefit from pinching, training.*

fall they may take cuttings to nurture along indoors during the winter. (See special feature, page 43.)

If you live in a cold-winter climate zone, you can cut the stems of many tender shrubs or perennials back to the main branches of the season's growth and set them in a sheltered area for protection from freezing. (Hardy plants may not need protection.) In mild-winter areas, cutting back the stems in spring stimulates vigorous, fresh growth and prevents woody and twiggy branches from forming.

Some plants will live through mild winters and even bloom intermittently, but you still might want to cut them back to prevent ranginess.

Hanging plants that grow equally well indoors and out can be brought inside for protection before the first winter frost.

Your ailing plant

Airborne plants are subject to attacks from pests and diseases just as plants on the ground are. But before you mount a campaign against them, consider the possibility that your plant is getting too much or too little water, food, or light as the reason for its poor health. And be sure to give a new plant a chance to adapt to its environment before deciding that something is wrong with it.

Plant problems

The symptoms of too much or too little water are often similar: wilted or dry leaves that yellow or brown and possibly drop. One way to check whether the plant is getting too much or too little water is to inspect the soil to see whether it's dry or moist. Don't just feel the soil at the top of the container; tap the plant out of the container and look at the soil by the roots. Often the soil at the bottom may be soggy while that at the top is dry, or the other way around.

Removing the plant for a quick soil check is also a good way to find out if the plant is pot bound. If so, the roots will show through the soil around the outside of the root ball. The common symptoms of crowded roots are a lack of plant growth and/or pale, sparse foliage. Loosen the crowded roots gently with your fingers and then repot the specimen in a larger container, or, with a sharp knife, carefully shave an inch or so off the root ball and put the plant back into its old container with a layer of new soil around the sides. (See pages 24-31 for complete planting instructions.)

While insufficient fertilizer may be signaled by slow growth or yellowing foliage and sparse, short-lived bloom, too much food can cause leaves to turn brown and crisp around the edges and kill tender new growth. To fertilize, follow the feeding instructions on page 39.

Too much light or sun is indicated by pale, wilted, or burned foliage. Spindly growth, sparse foliage, or dropping leaves can be signs of insufficient light. Check the location against the needs of the plant and relocate the plant if necessary.

Sudden chilly drafts or blasts of hot air can cause tender or delicate plants suddenly to drop their leaves or flowers.

Pests and insects

The insects and pests you'll have the most trouble with are those that travel by air and those that drop from overhead trees. But if your container isn't thoroughly cleaned or you've used unsterilized potting soil, the denizens who lived in the soil or pot before planting may give you trouble. Hanging plants are usually out of reach of snails, slugs, and other slow-moving or nonflying pests. Below are a few of the pests and insects you may encounter along with recommended measures for combating them:

Aphids. Tiny green, black, yellow, or pink insects. Live and feed in colonies; stunt growth; disfigure leaves, buds, flowers. Control: spray off with water; or apply pyrethrum (pyrethrins), malathion, or diazinon.

Leafhoppers. Small, fast-moving green or brownish insects. Feed on underside of leaf; cause white stippling. Control: same as for aphids.

Scale. Small insects that attach themselves to stems and leaves; generally have a protective shell; colony forming. Control: malathion and petroleum oils.

Spider mites. One of the worst summer pests. Signs are finely stippled leaves with silvery webs on underside. Use a hand lens to see the mites themselves. Controls: spray off with water; apply malathion, diazinon, petroleum oils, or specially formulated miticides, such as Kelthane.

Thrips. Tiny, fast-moving insects that damage plant tissue by rasping surface cells. Feed on inside flower buds and foliage and cause distortion or failure to open. Controls: pyrethrum, rotenone, malathion, or diazinon.

Whiteflies. Very small, common pests. Scalelike nymphs when young; feed on underside of leaves. Pure white adults flutter about erratically when plant is disturbed. Controls: sevin, malathion, diazinon, or petroleum oils.

Diseases

Many plant diseases are encouraged by moist, humid, warm air and poor circulation. Hanging plants often have the advantage of good air circulation if placed in an exposed location. But keep your eye on and regularly turn those plants hanging near walls or in corners.

Humidity-loving plants, *such as 'Fluffy Ruffles' fern, like a shower from water mister.*

Botrytis, gray mold. Soft decay of flowers, leaves, or stems, followed by blackened tissues covered with a downy, gray mold. Usually the fungus enters the plant through dead or dying flowers or leaves, but under the right conditions (cool, moist air; high humidity) it can infect live tissues. Controls: quick removal of dead plant parts and application of dicloran, benomyl, or thiram.

Mildew. Appears as a white or gray, powdery or mealy coating on leaves, tender stems, and flower buds. Encouraged by high humidity, crowding of plants, poor circulation, more shade than plant needs. Controls: benomyl, cycloheximide powder, or sulphur dust.

Rust. Appears first on undersides of leaves. Most common symptom is appearance of numerous yellow orange colored pustules or wartlike formations that eventually burst. Upper leaf surfaces may show mottled and yellowish areas. Rust survives winters on living plants and on dead leaves. Keep plants tidy; remove dead, dying leaves. Controls: ferbam or cycloheximide powder.

Indoor culture

Indoor hanging plants require basically the same care as outdoor hanging plants—watering, feeding, turning, the proper cultural conditions, and pest and disease control. Read the above sections on general care; they apply to both.

Because providing the proper amounts of light and growing conditions is just as important as watering and feeding, also read the section on situating a plant indoors (pages 14-16).

On pages 16-17 are lists of plants that are relatively easy to grow indoors. Other house plants are listed on pages 44-78. Many indoor plants prefer a tropical or near-tropical atmosphere with steady warmth and high humidity. You can provide humidity by spraying the foliage of the plant with a water mister or syringe. (Don't spray plants with hairy leaves and don't spray just before exposing a plant to direct sunlight.) Another way to provide humidity is to hang beneath the plant a dish or saucer with a moistened sponge on it. As the water in the sponge evaporates, it creates a moist atmosphere around the plant. Hang a dish and sponge beneath a plant just as you would hang a drip saucer beneath it (see page 34).

Providing steady warmth can be difficult, especially if you turn the heat off during the night or day. Avoid placing the plant near heating ducts or such appliances as a stove or television set; protect it from exposure to nighttime drafts from partly opened windows.

1. *Snip off 3 to 4-inch length of healthy stem with clippers, knife, finger nails. Take cuttings in spring or, from tender plants, in fall to nurture along indoors during winter and plant out in spring.*

Cuttings will give you more plants

One good way to increase your plant collection is with cuttings or "slips"—short lengths of stem taken from a "mother" plant. To root a slip, cut off the end of a healthy plant's stem; then place it in potting soil or a cup of water. Soon, roots will form—the stem is beginning its transformation to a full-fledged plant. Trading cuttings with friends is a good way to acquire new and different specimens.

Not all plants will grow from cuttings. Annuals and plants that have only one growing tip at the end of a central stem and plants that won't sprout new growth along the stems or from the base will not. But many perennials, shrubs, and vines (both indoor and outdoor types) *will* grow from cuttings. Some plants, particularly those with fleshy, tender stems, such as plectranthus, coleus, and wandering Jew, root faster than those with woodier stems, such as lantana and camellia.

2. *Strip lower leaves from cutting; poke about 1½ inches of stem into pot of soil mix. Some tender stems root if you just put them in water. Woody stems may benefit from root hormone sold at nurseries.*

3. *When roots establish (it may take anywhere from a few weeks to a few months, depending on the plant), transplant into larger container, and your cutting is on its way to becoming a full-sized plant.*

Plants That Like to Hang

On the following pages you'll find descriptions of numerous plants that grow attractively in hanging containers, along with tips on how to care for each. These include a wide selection of house plants, as well as common outdoor landscape and bedding plants. Many will grow equally well indoors during the winter and outdoors during the warm summer months.

The plants are listed by both their botanical and common names. A description of each appears under the botanical name (with cross references to it under the common name). Most botanical names have two parts: the first is the plant's genus name, the second indicates which species it is. (In cases where more than one species is described, the genus name is followed by the word "species.")

By no means should you feel limited to suspending just the plants listed here. Many other common plants will grow equally well in hanging containers. Since nurserymen constantly seem to be trying new ideas (and since different plants are more available in different parts of the country), you may well find exciting hanging plants not listed here. And of course you should feel free to experiment with your own ideas. (Many suggestions to spark your creativity are given in special features throughout this book.)

Don't be discouraged if your hanging plants tend to be more upright or spreading than you'd expected. Many plants take time for their branches to lengthen or become heavy with the weight of flowers before they droop. Even such common hangers as cascading petunias ('White Cascade', for instance) may tend to develop as much outward growth as trailing growth. You can help many of these reluctant plants to droop by attaching small weights to their branches, see page 42.

ABELIA grandiflora 'Prostrata'. Abelia has graceful, arching branches densely clothed with 1-inch, oval leaves, usually quite glossy and tinged bronze when new. It produces tubular, bell-like flowers in clusters at the ends of the branches and among the leaves during summer and early fall. It's partially deciduous, even in the mildest climates. Abelia grows and flowers best in the sun but will take some shade. To keep the plant form graceful, prune selectively; don't shear. The more stems you cut in winter or early spring, the more open and arching new growth will be.

ABUTILON megapotamicum (Flowering maple; Chinese bellflower). **House plant.** Abutilon's flowers, resembling red and yellow lanterns, gaily decorate long, rangy branches from May until about the first frost. It may bloom year round in mild climates. Abutilon enjoys moist soil and partial shade inland, full sun in cool climates. Apply complete fertilizer three times during the growing season. To prevent legginess and sparse foliage, cut back branches to hard wood each spring; pinch back new growth frequently. In cold climates bring plants indoors during winter.

ACHIMENES. House plant. A perennial, achimenes requires similar treatment to that given its relatives, the African violet and gloxinia. It has flaring, tubular flowers that reach 2 inches across. Since some types are upright, be sure to get a trailing variety. Plants need warmth and night temperatures not below 60°. In cool climates grow them indoors. Outdoors, in warmer areas, grow them in light shade and a protected location. Propagate the plants from rhizomes: in March-April place the rhizomes ½-1-inch deep in moist peat moss and sand. When new plants are 3 inches high, set 6 to 12 of them in a 6 to 7-inch fern pot or basket. Keep the soil moist but not wet, feeding the plants regularly for a long bloom. In fall, gradually withhold water to let them wither. Cure and dry the rhizomes and store them in a cool, dry place, repotting them in spring.

AECHMEA 'Foster's Favorite'. House plant. A bromeliad usually grown indoors except in mild summer and winter climates, this plant should be kept in a shaded location with good air circulation. It forms an open rosette of leathery, glossy, bright wine red leaves about 1 foot long. Flowers appear in drooping, spikelike clusters, coral red and blue in color. Place the plant in fast-draining but moisture-retentive soil to which you've added fir bark. Every week or two apply water to the cups in the leaves. Water the soil only when it's quite dry to the touch.

AEONIUM simsii. House plant. This low, dense, spreading succulent with yellow flowers takes full sun outdoors in mild summer and winter climates. Elsewhere, aeonium is used as a house plant. Provide good light if you hang them indoors. Let plants dry out slightly between waterings to allow air to penetrate the soil.

AESCHYNANTHUS SPECIES. House plant. Several species make fine trailers. *A. lobbianus*, commonly known as the "lipstick plant," has 2-inch-long tubular red flowers that form along the stems. Other species are *A. marmoratus*, grown for its green leaves mottled with maroon; *A. speciosus*, with bright yellow and orange flowers up to 4 inches long; and *A.* 'Splendens', with clusters of orange-red flowers tinged maroon. All species bloom intermittently throughout the year when grown as house plants. They need good light, high humidity, and high temperatures. Outdoors during the warm months, they will grow in a protected

Lipstick plant (Aeschynanthus) *is named for its flowers: foliage and form are like columnea's.*

and lightly shaded location. Plant them in loose, fibrous potting mix.

AFRICAN DAISY. See Osteospermum.

AIRPLANE PLANT. See Chlorophytum.

ALGERIAN IVY. See Hedera canariensis.

ALYSSUM saxatile (Basket-of-gold). This is a hardy perennial with dense clusters of tiny golden yellow flowers in spring and early summer. Variety 'Luteum' (often sold as 'Citrinum') has pale yellow flowers. Set plants in a wire basket with other sun-loving spring flowers. Or mass them alone in a box or pot and let them trail over the sides. Grow alyssum in full sun.

AMARACUS dictamnus (Crete dittany). An aromatic perennial herb with slender, arching stems to 1 foot long, this plant has attractive, thick, round, woolly leaves with a gray green color. The flowers range from pink to purple, are ½ inch long, and bloom in hoplike heads from summer to fall. The plants show best alone in a pot. Grow them in full sun or light shade.

AMETHYST FLOWER. See Browallia.

ARABIS caucasica 'Variegata' (Wall rockcress). Popular in rock gardens in cold-winter areas, this arabis variety has gray leaves with creamy white margins. Varieties 'Pink Charm' and 'Rosabella' have pink flowers. Flowers are at their best in spring. The plants form a low, spreading mat, making an attractive companion for *Alyssum saxatile* and aubrieta. Grow them in full sun; in hot, dry areas, provide light shade. Let the soil dry out slightly between waterings.

ARENARIA montana (Sandwort). Arenaria is a low-growing perennial that forms a dense mat of mosslike foliage with stems trailing to 1 foot. White, 1-inch flowers bloom profusely in late spring and early summer. Grow arenaria in part shade and moist soil.

ARTEMISIA schmidtiana 'Silver Mound'. The silvery white, finely cut leaves of this dwarf artemisia (plants

Pink, blue, *lavender, orchid, and purple flowers: features of achimenes, a house plant.*

Abelia, *a partially deciduous shrub, is often used as a ground cover; you can also try hanging it.*

grow just 12 inches high) will add texture and tone to baskets planted with red or orange flowers and blends beautifully with blues, lavenders, and pinks. The variety 'Nana' is even smaller than 'Silver Mound'—just 2 inches high. Grow these plants in full sun, keeping the soil slightly on the dry side.

ARTILLERY PLANT. See Pilea microphylla.

ASPARAGUS, ORNAMENTAL (Asparagus fern). **House plant.** These plants are valued mostly for their handsome foliage and interesting texture; some specimens do have small but fragrant flowers and colorful berries. (The name "fern" applied to these plants is incorrect, for they are not true ferns.)

Most ornamental asparagus look greenest in part shade but will grow in sun near the coast and in other cool-summer areas. The foliage turns yellow in dense shade or poor light. Asparagus ferns do well indoors in good light or outdoors on the patio or in another protected outdoor location. They survive light frosts but may be killed by severe cold. Plant them in well-drained soil with peat moss or ground bark. Provide ample water. Feed the plants in spring with a complete fertilizer. Trim out the old shoots to make room for new spring growth.

Basket asparagus (*A. crispus*) is an airy, graceful plant with bright green, three-angled leaves in whorls of three.

Another species called basket asparagus (*A. scandens*) is a slender, branching vine with needlelike leaves on drooping stems; it produces tiny, greenish white flowers and scarlet berries.

Myers asparagus (*A. densiflorus* 'Myers') has stiff stems (upright or spreading more than trailing), densely clothed with needlelike, deep green leaves that give a fluffy appearance.

Smilax asparagus (*A. asparagoides*) is a many-branched, vining plant with 1-inch-long, sharp-pointed leaves and small fragrant white flowers in spring, followed by blue berries.

Sprenger asparagus (*A. d.* 'Sprengeri') has arching, drooping stems 3 to 6 feet long, covered with bright green, 1-inch-long, needlelike leaves. It produces bright red berries.

AUBRIETA deltoidea. A low, spreading, and mat-forming perennial, aubrieta grows 2 to 6 inches high and 12 to 18 inches across. Its tiny flowers come in shades of red, lilac, or purple. It is effective in a combination with *Alyssum saxatile* and arabis. Grow the plant in full sun but provide some shade in hot areas.

AZALEA, EVERGREEN TYPES. Evergreen azaleas that are low growing and compact can put on a fine display of color in the air. Since azaleas can be demanding in their needs for particular climate conditions, choose types that will do well in your area.

There are about 11 groups of evergreen azaleas. Each includes a host of named varieties bred to thrive in different conditions. The following are a few you can hang:

Belgian Indica hybrids tolerate temperatures to 20° or 30° and have lush, full foliage and large flowers. In this group you might try 'Mme. Petrick', with cherry red, semi-double flowers from February through April; grow it in half sun.

Of the Gable hybrids that will tolerate temperatures to 0° is 'Purple Splendor', with 2-inch, crimson purple flowers in April.

'Aphrodite', a Glenn Dale hybrid, is hardy and has pale rose pink flowers in March and April; grow it in three-quarters sun.

The Kurume hybrids include 'Hino-crimson', which does well in half sun, is hardy to 5° or 10°, and has brilliant red flowers on flat, tiered branches from February through April.

In the Macrantha hybrid group are 'Flame Creeper', with orange red single flowers in April and May on low, spreading plants; 'Gumpo Pink' with rose pink flowers in May and June; and 'Rosaeflora', a very low-growing plant with rose pink double flowers during April and May.

Your nurseryman will probably carry the types most suitable for your area and can advise you on hybrids that will be attractive in hanging containers.

Azaleas require an acid soil and plenty of air around the roots. Plant them in loose, well-drained soil that's rich in organic matter. Place them slightly high and

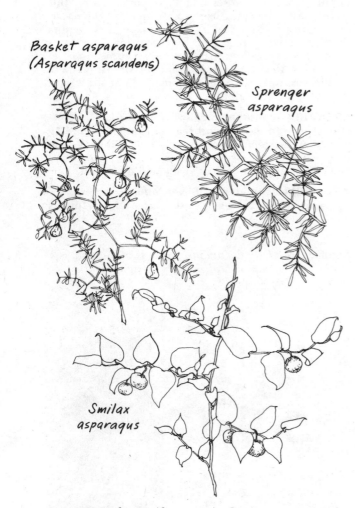

Basket asparagus
(Asparagus scandens)

Sprenger asparagus

Smilax asparagus

Asparagus ferns (*from top*): *Sprenger asparagus, basket asparagus, and smilax asparagus.*

don't put soil around the stems or trunks. Azaleas like plenty of moisture, but you shouldn't let the soil become soggy. Fertilize them when growth starts in the spring, at bloom time or immediately afterward, and repeat the process monthly until August. Use an acid fertilizer, following directions carefully, or cut recommended portions in half and feed twice as often. Sun and shade tolerance of azaleas differs according to varieties. An ideal location for many is in the filtered shade of tall trees. East and north exposures are the next best. Dense shade causes the plants to become lanky and to bloom sparsely.

BABY'S TEARS. See Pilea depressa and Soleirolia.

BASKET-OF-GOLD. See Alyssum saxatile.

BEAR'S FOOT FERN. See Humata.

BEGONIA SPECIES. Best grown in cool-summer areas with mild winters, begonias are fine hanging basket plants and very beautiful, especially the tuberous begonias with long pendent stems and the fibrous begonias. Some are raised as house plants in areas where outdoor conditions are unsuitable..

In general, begonias perform best in filtered shade, in a moist temperate atmosphere, and in soil that is fast draining and slightly acid. Provide ample water and consistent feeding, at first with a high-nitrogen fertilizer and, when blooms appear, with a low-nitrogen fertilizer, such as a 2-10-10.

Elatior hybrids (crosses between tuberous begonias and winter-blooming bulbous begonias) are usually grown as house plants for their winter flowers. Provide plenty of light but not direct sun. Water when the top inch of soil is dry. Keep water off the leaves. Cut back to 4-inch stubs when plants become rangy.

Of the cane-stemmed begonia varieties, *B.* 'Pink Rubra', which has slender, arching stems and bright green, angel-wing leaves, is a good choice.

A fibrous-rooted begonia, *B.* 'Richmondensis', has arching stems and leaves that are a deep green on top and reddish underneath. Its flowers are salmon pink in color. It will grow indoors where frosts are severe, outdoors elsewhere. Outdoors locate the plants in filtered shade or sun if temperatures are cool.

B. tuberhybrida 'Pendula' is the spectacular tuberous begonia with large flowers in just about every imaginable shade of pink, red, rose, orange, yellow, salmon, and white; some specimens come bicolored. Flowers grow at the ends of long, pendulous stems. Flower forms are usually double and indicated as ruffled, rose, picotee, and carnation, with plain, ruffled, or frilled petals. Many cultivated varieties are available, the names usually indicating flower color. Just be sure to get the 'Pendula' types that will trail.

Grow begonias in filtered shade, protecting them from the wind. Water tuberous begonias regularly, but don't let the soil become soggy. Water in the morning: damp foliage at night encourages mildew. In dry climates, provide humidity with an overhead fog nozzle and hose. After bloom period withhold water as leaves start turning yellow. When foliage is entirely yellow, dig up the tubers, wash off soil, and remove the stems; then cure the tubers in sun for several days. Store them in a cool, frost-free location for winter until planting time in spring.

BELOPERONE guttata (Shrimp plant). **House plant.** This indoor/outdoor shrub has small, tubular flowers, white with purple spots, enclosed in coppery bronze, overlapping bracts that form compact, drooping spikes 3 to 7 inches long. These spikes resemble large shrimp. The 'Chartreuse' variety has chartreuse yellow spikes.

Train the plant in its early stages by continued pinching into a bushy mound that arches over the sides of the container. When the plant reaches the desired compactness and shape, stop pinching it and let it bloom. To encourage bushiness, cut the stems back when the flower bracts turn black. This plant will take full sun, but its bracts and foliage fade unless it's grown in partial shade. The leaves may drop in cold weather (bring the plant indoors) or if the soil is too wet or too dry.

BILLBERGIA nutans (Queen's tears). **House plant.** Billbergia is often grown on bark slabs with the roots wrapped in sphagnum moss and leaf mold (see planting instructions under *Platycerium*). The plant has slender green leaves to 1½ feet long and spectacular spikes of rose red bracts and drooping flowers with green petals edged deep blue. It grows best in filtered shade and in light porous soil, needs little water during the winter when growth is slow, but requires large quantities of water during active growth in the warm season. Bring the plant indoors during winter and place it in a sunny window.

BLACK-EYED SUSAN VINE. See Thunbergia alata.

Like large shrimp, *the flower spikes of beloperone (a house plant) are coppery bronze in color.*

Tips on shopping for plants

House plants are sold in various stages of maturity. Outdoor shrubs, perennials, and vines usually come in gallon cans. Annuals and bedding plants generally are sold in flats or plastic cell packs ("pony packs"). Annuals, often in bloom, also may be available in small plastic pots. Both indoor and outdoor plants may be sold in hanging arrangements. Generally, you'll pay more for plants that are mature, in bloom, or ready to hang than you will for plants not displayed as hangers. Below are tips for selecting a healthy plant:

• Try to avoid plants with yellowish, discolored, sparse, stunted foliage and those with leggy stems. A few poor leaves usually won't matter, but do watch for an overall unhealthy appearance.

• Pass up flowers in flats or cell packs already in bloom; choose younger ones that haven't yet budded out.

• Avoid pot bound plants whose roots show through the container's drain hole.

Casual and bushy, *campanula has blue or white flowers; plant several for a full effect.*

BLEEDING HEART GLORYBOWER. See Clerodendrum.

BLUE MARGUERITE. See Felicia.

BOSTON FERN. See Nephrolepis exaltata.

BOUGAINVILLEA. Best in warm-winter climates having infrequent frosts and relatively high average temperatures, bougainvillea is adaptable to colder areas if given winter protection or if treated as a summer annual.

Of the many named varieties, those suited for hanging containers are the shrubby types, such as 'Crimson Jewel', 'La Jolla' (bright red), and 'Temple Fire' (bronze red). Provide a warm location in direct sun against a south-facing wall or grow in filtered shade in extremely hot areas. Give plants plenty of water and fertilize regularly during the growing season. Pinch frequently while plants are young to encourage full, bushy specimens.

BOUVARDIA longiflora 'Albatross'. House plant. Bouvardia is an evergreen shrub having fragrant, snow white, 3-inch-long tubular flowers in loose clusters on weak stems. Pinch out stem tips to encourage bushiness. Occasionally cut back flowering branches to stimulate new growth. This is an indoor/outdoor plant that requires good light.

BRIDAL VEIL. See Tripogandra.

BROWALLIA SPECIES (Amethyst flower). A perennial usually grown as an annual, browallia will live over the winter if brought indoors. Lobelialike or petunialike blue, violet, or white flowers appear in clusters. The blue flowers usually have white throats or eyes. There are two species: *B. americana* (often

listed as *B. elata*), with branching stems and ½-inch flowers, and *B. speciosa*, which has a sprawling form and 1½ to 2-inch petunialike flowers. The plants need warmth and moisture: grow them in warm shade or filtered sun.

BUSY LIZZIE. See Impatiens.

CALCEOLARIA integrifolia. This calceolaria species is shrubby, with loose clusters of ½-inch, pouchlike flowers. Colors are red through red brown, orange, and pure yellow—as in 'Golden Nugget'. It takes full sun and heat and blooms best when pot bound.

CAMELLIA SPECIES. Many named varieties of the Sasanqua camellia (*C. sasanqua*) are spreading and vinelike. Of these low-growing Sasanquas, you might try 'Mine-No-Yuke' ('White Doves'), with large, white, peony-type double flowers and a willowy form; 'Tanya', which has deep rose pink single flowers and thrives in high heat and sun; and 'White Frills', which has semi-double, frilled white flowers.

A few Hiemalis camellias (*C. hiemalis*) are also low and spreading: try 'Showa-No-Sakae', with its arching branches, fast growth, and pink, semi-double or double flowers that are often marked with white.

Camellias need well-drained soil rich in organic matter. Plant them so that the base of the trunk is slightly above the soil line. Keep the soil moist but not soaking wet. In hot, dry spells, sprinkle the leaves with water. In the months before buds set and after bloom has ended, feed them with an acid commercial fertilizer high in nitrogen. As soon as buds set, begin feeding with a fertilizer low in nitrogen, say a 0-10-10 blend. Prune camellias after flowering. Remove dead or weak wood. Thin buds when they are so crowded that flowers can't open.

Definitely trailing, *ceropegia has white-marbled leaves on long stems; grows indoors or out.*

Young spider plant *(Chlorophytum) will later send out long runners on which baby plants will grow.*

CAMPANULA isophylla (Italian bellflower). This campanula species has trailing stems to 2 feet long, heart-shaped light green leaves, and profuse, star-shaped flowers in late summer and fall. Pale blue flowers (as on the variety 'Mayi') are common; 'Alba' has white flowers. Try two or three specimens of blue and white varieties together in a wooden box.

Campanulas are perennials usually grown as indoor/outdoor plants in cold-winter climates or, in mild areas, year round outdoors in filtered shade or full sun. The stems may die back after flowering. Plant campanulas in a well-drained potting mix. Start the seeds in spring or early summer for fall bloom the following year or propagate the plants from cuttings or divisions. Established young plants are frequently available at nurseries during spring, early summer.

CARDINAL CLIMBER. See Quamoclit.

CARISSA grandiflora 'Horizontalis'. House plant. Dense foliage and 2-inch, 5-petaled white flowers with the fragrance of star jasmine characterize this shrub. (Also try other trailing varieties, such as 'Green Carpet' and 'Minima'.)An indoor/outdoor candidate,*C. grandiflora* varieties require winter warmth and protection from frosts. Provide filtered shade in very hot summer areas and full sun elsewhere.

CATHARANTHUS roseus (Madagascar periwinkle). Often sold as *Vinca rosea.* A bushy perennial usually grown as an annual, this plant produces phloxlike flowers about 1½ inches wide in white, pink, and rose (or white with a red center, as in the variety 'Bright Eyes'). It will bush out over the sides of a container to spill slightly downward. Plants may live over the winter in mild areas but tend to become scraggly. It blooms best in hot climates during the summer and

fall. Plants started from seeds early indoors will bloom the first season; young plants are also available from nurseries. Grow Madagascar periwinkle in full sun or partial shade. Provide plenty of water, feed regularly.

CERASTIUM tomentosum (Snow-in-summer). A perennial ground cover, cerastium produces spreading, dense, tufty mats of silvery gray, ¾-inch-long leaves, and masses of small white flowers in early summer. It takes full sun—light shade in hot climates.

CEROPEGIA woodii (Rosary vine; string of hearts). **House plant.** Ceropegia is a succulent with long, thin, trailing stems covered with ⅔-inch-long, neatly paired leaves that are heart-shaped, thick, and fleshy, usually dark green and marbled with white. Some varieties may have larger leaves. The flowers are interesting but not showy. New plants can be started from small tubers forming on the stems. Grow ceropegia as a house plant or indoor/outdoor plant. Outdoors provide shade; indoors grow it in good light. Let the soil dry out slightly between waterings.

CHINESE BELLFLOWER. See Abutilon.

CHLOROPHYTUM comosum (Spider plant; airplane plant). **House plant.** This is a fascinating and unique plant that forms a cluster of arching, curved leaves 1 to 3 feet long, shaped like long, broad blades of grass and light green in color. (On *C. c. marginalis* the leaves are margined with white.) The spider plant's greatest attraction is its production of baby plants (just like the mother, complete with roots) on long, freely trailing stems. These plantlets can be pinched off and potted individually. When you buy the plant from a nursery or plant shop, it may not yet have produced offspring. White, ½-inch flowers appear in loose leafy-tipped

Clerodendrum, *a large, shrubby house or patio plant, has 7-inch leaves, scarlet flowers in fall.*

Squirrel's foot fern (Davallia) *sends out fronds from furry rhizomes that creep over soil surface.*

Grape ivy (Cissus rhombifolia) *has glossy leaves; it grows in high or low light intensity indoors or out.*

spikes above the foliage. Easy to grow indoors, spider plants like well-lighted windows. Outdoors, in warm-summer areas, they prefer light or filtered shade.

CHRISTMAS CACTUS. See Schlumbergera.

CISSUS SPECIES. House plant. Grape ivy (*C. rhombifolia*), with its tooth-edged, dark green leaves showing bronze overtones and divided into 1 to 4-inch-long leaflets, is probably best known as a tough house plant that takes either high or low light intensity. Two other species are also popular: kangaroo vine (*C. antarctica*), with shiny, medium green leaves 2 to 3½ inches long and almost as wide; and *C. discolor*, with bright-colored 6-inch leaves, toothed around the edges. All species require similar culture and like a well-drained soil that is not constantly damp.

CLERODENDRUM thomsoniae (Bleeding heart glory-bower). **House plant.** Clerodendrum is an evergreen, shrubby vine grown as an indoor/outdoor plant (outdoors year round in warm-winter climates). Its 4 to 7-inch, dark, shiny green leaves are oval and distinctly ribbed. Flowers appearing in flattish, 5-inch-wide clusters from August to October are scarlet, 1-inch tubes surrounded by large, ¾-inch white calyxes. The plant needs rich, loose, well-drained soil and plenty of moisture. Feed it regularly. Prune it back after flowering; protect it from frost.

COLEUS blumei. House plant. Many varieties and hybrids of coleus, the familiar bedding and house plant with brilliantly colored leaves, have long, branching stems that make them suitable for hanging. Leaves are often reddish, tinged green. On the variety 'Trailing Queen', the leaves are chartreuse to green along the edges and purplish to carmine in the center.

Indoors or out, the leaf color is best in strong,

Plants for foliage

The following plants have long, trailing stems, interesting foliage texture, or multi-colored leaves. Other foliage plants are shown on pages 60–61.

ASPARAGUS FERN. Lush green, nicely textured foliage; trailing habit. Sun or light shade.

CEROPEGIA (rosary vine). Thin, trailing stems.

CHLOROPHYTUM (spider plant). Long, trailing runners carry baby plants; indoors or outdoors.

CISSUS. Two varieties have ivylike habit: *C. rhombifolia* (grape ivy); *C. antarctica* (kangaroo vine).

COLEUS. Varieties have brilliantly colored leaves.

CYMBALARIA (kenilworth ivy). Trailing stems; variegated, kidney-shaped leaves.

EUONYMUS FORTUNEI 'GRACILIS'. Trailing habit.

FICUS. Several species with viny leaves and habit.

FITTONIA. Low, creeping; green, red-veined leaves.

GYNURA (velvet plant). Brilliant purple leaves.

HEDERA (ivy). Trailing habit, various leaf shapes.

LOTUS. Silvery gray, finely divided leaves.

LYSIMACHIA (creeping Jennie). Round, neatly paired, rich green leaves on trailing stems.

MARANTA (prayer plant). Spreading more than trailing; interesting foliage with unique markings.

PEPEROMIA. Several species with roundish, variegated leaves on short stems. House plant.

PHILODENDRON OXYCARDIUM. Trailing stems, large leaves.

PLECTRANTHUS (creeping Charlie). Easy to grow; shiny green leaves on thickly trailing stems.

SEDUM MORGANIANUM (donkey tail). Long, trailing stems resemble braided rope in texture.

SENECIO. Two species are trailing: *S. mikanioides* (German ivy) and *S. rowleyanus* (string of beads).

SYNGONIUM. Resembles philodendron. Arrowlike leaves, often variegated. House plant.

TOLMIEA (piggy-back plant). Lush green leaves rise from centers of older leaves. House plant.

TRADESCANTIA (wandering Jew). Trailing stems with green leaves often marked with white.

ZEBRINA (wandering Jew). Similar to tradescantia except that leaves are variegated purple, white, pink.

---

indirect light. Outdoors, plants will take some sun, but their colors tend to fade. Protect the plants from cool temperatures by bringing them indoors during the winter. Coleus is most often grown as a full-time house plant. Keep the soil evenly moist; feed the plant regularly with a high-nitrogen fertilizer.

To encourage branching, pinch the stems regularly. To keep growth vigorous, pinch off insignificant flower spikes as they appear. Propagate the plants by cutting off stems and putting them in water to root. When roots form, pot cuttings in loose, well-drained soil.

COLUMNEA SPECIES. House plants. Many columnea species have trailing stems that can grow to several feet long. *C.* 'Stavanger' has neat pairs of rounded, shiny, ½-inch leaves and 3 to 4-inch-long red tubular flowers with flaring mouths. *C. gloriosa* sports purplish leaves and 3-inch-long red flowers with yellow throats. *C. hirta* has small oval leaves and vermilion flowers with orange markings. *C. microphylla* features red flowers and coppery leaves with hairy surfaces. *C.* 'Flava' has bright yellow flowers.

Generally grown as house plants, columnea is related to African violets and prefers the same culture but a slightly lower temperature (55° to 60°). Columneas like humidity and bloom best when their roots are crowded. Plant them in a soil that is composed of 3 parts leaf mold, 1 part loam, ½ part sand, and a small amount of bone meal. Or use an African violet potting mix. Allow the soil surface to become dry to the touch between waterings. Feed the plants with a slightly acid fertilizer every two to four weeks. Do not feed when the soil is dry.

CONVOLVULUS SPECIES. Two convolvulus species are suitable for hanging containers: *C. mauritanicus* (ground morning glory) and *C. tricolor* (dwarf morning glory). Ground morning glory is a perennial with trailing stems to 3 feet covered with roundish, ½ to 1½-inch leaves and lavender blue, 1 to 2-inch flowers from June through November. The plant likes full sun and well-drained, gravelly soil.

Dwarf morning glory is a bushy, branching annual. Named varieties may be available: 'Crimson Monarch', with dark red flowers, and 'Royal Ensign', with bright blue flowers having yellow throats and white markings. The plant needs sun and warmth and blooms best when the soil is kept slightly on the dry side. Nick the seed coats with a sharp knife to hasten germination if you grow plants from seeds.

COTONEASTER SPECIES. Of the many cotoneaster species, try *C. adpressa* (creeping cotoneaster), a slow-growing deciduous shrub with pinkish flowers and bright red fruit, and *C. dammeri* (bearberry cotoneaster), a low, vigorous evergreen with white flowers and red fruit. Both bloom in the spring, later producing attractive fruits. They prefer poor soil slightly on the dry side and full sun.

CRASSULA SPECIES. House plant. Crassula is a large genus of which the common jade plant is a member. Several species have trailing, spreading stems. They are usually grown as house plants or as indoor/outdoor specimens. Though they take shade, they bloom best if given some sun.

C. imperialis has spreading branches and pointed leaves in groups of four surrounding the stem. The flowers are small.

C. lycopodioides is leafy and branching, like *C. imperialis*, but more delicate and not as full.

C. marginalis has reddish flowers and succulent, heart-shaped, flattish leaves.

C. perforata has thin stems with opposite pairs of triangular leaves. Its flowers are yellow.

Lobelia (*L. erinus* 'Hamburgia')

Airborne color

Just imagine solid masses of beautiful flowers striking you right at eye level. A sampling of the flowering plants you can hang appear on these pages. (See the special feature, page 55, for others.)

Many flowering hangers (such as lobelia, impatiens, and browallia) are common bedding plants available at the nursery during spring and summer. Dwarf varieties of many of these plants are usually scaled better for containers.

Besides bedding plants, many shrubs and perennials are nicely displayed in the air. Lipstick plants will bloom intermittently year-round when grown indoors. *Sedum sieboldii* bursts with pink in the fall. Azalea puts on an incomparable show when well tended.

Lipstick plant (*Aeschynanthus*)

Impatiens, Elfin strain (*I. walleriana*)   Browallia (*B. americana*)

Evergreen azalea 'Red Bird'

Sedum sieboldii

C. perfossa, called string-of-buttons, has thick leaves. At first erect, the stems become drooping in time. The flowers are small and yellow.

CREEPING CHARLIE. See Plectranthus.

CREEPING FIG. See Ficus pumila.

CREEPING JENNIE. See Lysimachia.

CRETE DITTANY. See Amaracus.

CUP FLOWER, DWARF. See Nierembergia.

CYANOTIS SPECIES (Kitten's ears). **House plant.** Two cyanotis species are hanging container candidates: *C. kewensis* and *C. somaliensis*. Both have fleshy, fuzzy, triangular leaves. *C. kewensis* has violet blue flowers; *C. somaliensis* has reddish, densely clustered flowers. They are both indoor/outdoor plants but flower best outdoors in the sun. Related to wandering Jew they may occasionally be sold under that name.

CYMBALARIA muralis (Kenilworth ivy). **House plant.** This is a perennial frequently grown as a house plant or outdoors in the shade as an annual. The stems are trailing and covered with small, kidney-shaped leaves having 3 to 7 toothlike lobes and flowers resembling tiny snapdragons in lilac blue, marked with white and yellow, on stalks slightly longer than the leaves. Kenilworth ivy flowers from spring to fall and likes moist soil. It's winter hardy in mild climates.

DAVALLIA trichomanoides (Squirrel's foot fern). **House plant.** Davallia is a fern with furry rhizomes that creep over the surface of a moss-lined basket, sending out finely divided fronds about 6 inches wide and growing to 12 inches long. Grow the plant indoors or outside during the summer (outdoors year round in warm-winter climates—it's hardy to 30°). It requires good light indoors, partial shade outdoors. Feed it occasionally. (For a similar fern, see *Humata*.)

DONKEY TAIL. See Sedum morganianum.

DRYOPTERIS SPECIES (Wood fern). Often found in nurseries in the Pacific coast states, *Dryopteris arguta*, or California wood fern, has dark green, finely cut fronds to 2½ feet. *D. dilatata*, or spreading wood fern, has many named varieties with fine fronds. Provide partial sun and keep the soil slightly on the dry side; be careful not to water too frequently.

EASTER CACTUS. See Rhipsalidopsis.

ENGLISH IVY. See Hedera helix.

EPIPHYLLUM (Orchid cactus). **House plant.** Grown as a house plant or as an indoor/outdoor plant in areas where summer temperatures are mildly warm, epiphyllum has arching or trailing stems that are long, flat, and smooth. (Outdoors, provide broken shade and protect it from frost.) Flowers to 10 inches across appear from April through June on the stalks. Colors range from white, cream, yellow, and pink to lavender, scarlet, and orange. Some varieties offer blends of two or more colors.

Plant the orchid cactus in rich, quick-draining soil with plenty of leaf mold, peat moss or ground bark, and sand. Be careful not to over water; this may cause buds to drop. Feed the plant with low-nitrogen, high-phosphate fertilizer before and after it blooms.

EPISCIA cupreata (Flame violet). **House plant.** A relative of African violets, this house plant is low growing, has 4-inch oval leaves that usually develop a deep coppery color (named varieties such as 'Metallica' and 'Viridifolia' may have striped leaves with colored edges). Its flowers resemble long-tubed, orange red African violets. The plant needs high humidity, temperatures between 60° and 70°, and good indirect light. Use the soil recommended for columnea and follow the same directions for feeding and watering.

ERIGERON karvinskianus (Fleabane). Often sold as *Vittadinia*. This is a graceful, trailing perennial with 1-inch-long leaves, often toothed at the tips, and dainty, ¾-inch flowers with many pink or white rays. Grow it in fast-draining sandy soil and sun or light shade. Trim back the stems after flowering to prolong the bloom period.

EUONYMUS fortunei 'Gracilis'. Choose this euonymus variety if you want one with a trailing habit that is less vigorous and more restrained than other types. Grown for its foliage, texture, and form, 'Gracilis' has rich, dark green leaves variegated with white or cream, the light portions turning pinkish in cold weather. It's hardy and evergreen below 0°. Grow the plant in full sun or partial shade.

EUPHORBIA myrsinites. Euphorbia's stems are somewhat floppy and angle outward from the base of the plant, rising upward slightly. Clusters of flower bracts are flattish and chartreuse to yellow in winter and early spring. The blue gray leaves are stiff, roundish, and set closely around the stems. An evergreen perennial, euphorbia withstands cold and heat but is short-lived in warm-winter climates.

Orchid cactus *(Epiphyllum) is a succulent with arching stems and large blooms.*

EVERGREEN GRAPE. See Rhoicissus.

FELICIA amelloides (Blue marguerite). A shrubby perennial (but not the true marguerite, *Chrysanthemum frutescens*), blue marguerite grows to about 1 foot tall and spreads to 2 or 3 feet. The foliage is rather rough and aromatic. Daisy flowers are 1¼ inches wide and sky blue with yellow centers. Plants bloom almost continuously in mild winters if dead flowers are removed to stimulate new ones. In late summer, prune stems back to hard wood to encourage new blooming wood. (Plants tend to become rangy if not pruned.) Several named varieties may be available with large, rich blue flowers. Grow blue marguerites in a sunny outdoor location.

FERNS. (See *Davallia*, squirrel's foot fern; *Dryopteris*, wood fern; *Humata*, bear's foot fern; *Nephrolepis*, Boston ferns; *Pellaea*, roundleaf fern; *Platycerium*, staghorn fern; *Polypodium*, hare's foot fern; *Pyrrosia*, Japanese felt fern. The asparagus fern is not a true fern: see Asparagus, ornamental, page 46.)

FICUS SPECIES. House plant. Creeping fig (*F. pumila*) is an evergreen vine related to the fig tree and rubber plant. It grows well indoors or out, in sun or shade, and in low or high light intensity. When young, the leaves are neat and heart-shaped; on older plants they become leathery and oblong. Set several plants in a container to create a full effect. Water them regularly.

Mistletoe fig (*F. diversifolia*), also a house plant, is a slow grower with twisting open branches and thick, roundish, dark green leaves stippled with tan and black. Small, greenish yellow fruits are borne continuously. Grow it in part shade or diffused sunlight.

FITTONIA verschaffeltii. House plant. Fittonia is a low, creeping house plant with handsome, dark green, oval-shaped, 4-inch leaves veined with red. One variety, 'Argyroneura', has white veins. Provide north light, high humidity, and a warm, even temperature. Cut stems can be rooted in water and then potted.

FLAME VIOLET. See Episcia.

FLEABANE. See Erigeron.

FLOWERING MAPLE. See Abutilon.

FRAGARIA SPECIES (Strawberry). Most of the strawberries will produce well in the air—just be sure to water them often and deeply. Grow the plants in full sun. The planting season is usually early spring (when plants are available at nurseries) or in the fall in mild climates for a winter crop if you've chosen an edible type. Plant carefully: the crown (where the stems meet the roots) should be just above the soil level when planted. Many varieties are available; they are often bred to tolerate various climate conditions or to resist diseases and pests. The types sold in your nursery should be well adapted to your area. Pick the strawberries when they are full and red; feed the plants after the first crop.

FUCHSIA hybrida. Fuchsias perform best in areas with cool summer temperatures and a moist atmosphere. Outside of these areas, they may be difficult to grow. In full bloom, the flowers cover the plants from early summer to the first frost. Color combinations are many. The sepals (the top parts of the flowers that flare back) are almost always white, red, or pink. The corolla (the inside bell-like part) may be almost any possible color within the range of white, blue violet, purple, pink, red, and shades approaching orange. Flower sizes and forms are equally varied.

Fuchsia forms range from erect types from 3 to 12 feet tall to trailing types (along with a full range in between). For hanging, you will need trailing types or

---

Plants for flower color

Many of the flowering plants listed below are common bedding plants; others are shrubs or perennials. A few can be grown indoors. (Also see pages 52–53.)

AESCHYNANTHUS (lipstick plant). Intermittent bloom year-round when grown indoors.

ALYSSUM (basket-of-gold). Golden yellow spring and early summer flowers. Sun loving.

CALCEOLARIA. Warm-colored, pouchlike flowers.

CAMPANULA (Italian bellflower). White or blue starlike flowers in summer and fall. Sun or light shade.

CATHARANTHUS (*Vinca rosea*). Bedding plant with red, pink, and white summer flowers.

EPIPHYLLUM (orchid cactus). Spring bloom; wide color range. Grows indoors or out.

GAZANIA. Daisylike flowers in late spring, early summer.

IMPATIENS. Red to white summer flowers.

IPOMOEA (morning glory). Funnel-shaped red, white, or blue summer flowers. Grow in sun.

LANTANA. Wide color range, long bloom period.

LATHYRUS (sweet pea). Wonderfully fragrant flowers in many colors. Likes sun.

LOBELIA. Popular bedding plant with tiny flowers in many shades of blue. Light shade or sun.

NEMESIA. Spring-blooming flowers in mixed colors.

OSTEOSPERMUM (trailing African daisy). Daisylike flowers in spring (year-round in mild areas).

PELARGONIUM (geranium). Popular garden plant; use trailing types (see page 65). Grow in sun, light shade.

PETUNIA. Common bedding plant for summer bloom in wide color range. Grow in sun.

RHIPSALIDOPSIS (Easter cactus). Spring flowers; grows well indoors.

SAXIFRAGA (strawberry geranium). House plant with loose, open flower clusters.

SCHLUMBERGERA (Christmas cactus). Good house plant for winter bloom.

TROPAEOLUM (nasturtium). Summer flowers in red through cream, many bicolors.

VINCA. Bluish spring flowers. Shade or part sun.

VIOLA (pansy, violet). Ever popular for spring and early summer flowers.

those that can be trained to trail by pinching and pruning. Several longtime favorite varieties are 'Red Spider', 'Swingtime', 'Marinka', and 'First Love'. In choosing a fuchsia to hang, ask your nurseryman for suggestions; many types are bred to tolerate heat, low humidity, and other adverse conditions.

Locate your fuchsias where they will be cool and protected from the wind. They like morning sun and afternoon shade or day-long, dappled shade. Plant them in soil mix that is fast draining but water retentive. If the weather is warm and dry, provide humidity and moisture by frequently sprinkling the foliage with water or spraying it with a fogger nozzle on the end of a garden hose.

Water as often as you can: it's almost impossible to overwater thriving fuchsias growing in well-drained containers and soil. Apply light doses of a complete fertilizer every 10 days to 2 weeks or follow the directions on the label.

If plants begin growing leggier than you wish, pinch out tips of branches to force growth into side branching. Pick off old flowers as they begin to fade; never allow berries to form after blooms drop.

Where frosts are light, fuchsias tend to lose their leaves; sometimes tender growth is killed. Hard frosts will kill plants back to hard wood or even roots. If you live in a severe winter area, hold the plants over by storing them indoors in bins or boxes of sawdust (40° to 50° is ideal). Keep them moist but not soggy.

If you live in a frost-free area, in early spring cut out approximately the volume of growth that formed the previous summer—leave about two healthy leaf buds on each twig of growth. If you're in a mild-frost area, cut out frost-damaged wood and remove most of the last summer's growth. If yours is a cold-winter area, prune lightly (remove leaves and twiggy growth) before storing. Then in the spring, prune out broken branches, cutting back into live wood.

GARDENIA jasminoides 'Radicans'. Gardenias in hanging containers? Some are perfectly suitable. The 'Radicans' variety grows only 6 to 12 inches high and spreads 2 to 3 feet. It has small, dark green leaves, often streaked with white, and summer flowers 1 inch wide but still with the form and fragrance of other larger varieties.

To perform well, gardenias need ample warmth and water and steady feeding. Though hardy to 20°, they will not bloom well without summer warmth. If you live in a cool region, grow them in full sun; in a hot area, place them in filtered shade or morning sun and afternoon shade. In a desert region, give them a north or east exposure.

Plant gardenias in fast-draining, moisture-retentive soil, placing them slightly high in the new containers so that soil is not around the stems. Avoid crowding more than one plant into a container. Keep the soil moist. Excessive salts in the water may burn the leaves. Feed the plants every three to four weeks during the growing season with an acid plant food. Prune to remove scraggly branches and faded flowers.

GAZANIA SPECIES. Gazania's bold, daisylike flowers offer a dazzling display during the late spring and early summer. (In mild climates the plants may bloom intermittently throughout the year.) Both clumping types (complex hybrids) and trailing species (G. leucolaena, G. uniflora) may be available. Clumping gazanias may be used and have a wide range of bright flower colors (some bicolors), but the trailing forms with long stems are the most suitable. Grow gazanias in full sun or part shade during the hottest part of the day. Carry gazanias through harsh winters by taking cuttings in the fall to root in vermiculite and pot up in the spring. Nurseries usually carry young plants during the spring.

GERANIUM. See Pelargonium.

GERMAN IVY. See Senecio mikanioides.

GOLDFISH PLANT. See Hypocyrta.

GRAPE IVY. See Cissus rhombifolia.

GROUND MORNING GLORY. See Convolvulus mauritanicus.

GYNURA SPECIES (Velvet plant). **House plant.** Two gynura species (G. aurantiaca and G. sarmentosa) are house plants having toothed, lance-shaped leaves thickly covered with violet or purple hairs that give them brilliant color and a velvety appearance and feel. G. sarmentosa has toothed-edged leaves, reddish on the underside. The leaves may grow to 6 inches long and 2½ inches wide. Plants are shrubby and can spill to 3 feet. Flowers are insignificant; pinch them out as they form to keep plants vigorous. Grow gynura in strong, indirect sunlight.

HARE'S FOOT FERN. See Polypodium aureum.

HEDERA SPECIES (Ivy). **House plant.** Algerian ivy (H. canariensis) and English ivy (H. helix) will trail in hanging containers. Algerian ivy has shiny, rich green

Plump and juicy, *ripening strawberries spill over the edge of a hanging clay pot.*

leaves 5 to 8 inches wide with 3 to 5 shallow lobes. Leaves are more widely spaced on stems than on English ivy. Plants also require more moisture than English ivy.

Tough and adaptable to a wide range of indoor conditions, the named varieties of *Hedera helix* have small, interesting leaves and growth forms ranging from bushy to vinelike. 'Hahn's Self-Branching' is branching, with 1½-inch, light green leaves; 'Needlepoint' has dark green leaves with deeply pointed lobes. Other varieties, such as 'Glacier' and 'Marginata', have variegated leaves. Varieties are often sold under different names in different nurseries and plant shops.

The hedera ivies will grow with little light in both cool and warm atmospheres as long as the daily temperature fluctuations are not too great. Keep the soil moist and spongy to the touch, checking periodically to see that it's damp down by the roots (page 41). Feed the plants once every two months, especially during the winter. Check regularly for red spider mite. Frequent misting with water may help to discourage these insects.

HELIOTROPE. See Heliotropium.

HELIOTROPIUM arborescens (Heliotrope). A perennial usually grown for seasonal color and fragrance, heliotrope will tend to spill over the sides of a hanging container, especially as the stems grow longer and the flower spikes open. Flowers are dark violet to white and arranged in tightly grouped, curved, and one-sided spikes that form massive rounded clusters. Start with small, soft-stemmed plants; older ones are slow to reach a drooping form. Heliotrope takes sun or partial shade in hot-summer climates. Bring the plant indoors or protect it from the cold during the winter. Let the soil dry out slightly between waterings.

HELXINE. See Soleirolia.

HERBS. (See *Amaracus*, Crete dittany; *Rosmarinus*, rosemary; *Thymus*, thyme. Also see special feature about herbs on page 10.)

HONEY BELL. See Mahernia.

HOYA SPECIES (Wax flower; wax plant). **House plant.** A group of vinelike or shrubby house plants, hoyas have thick, waxy, evergreen leaves and tight clusters of small, waxy flowers.

Hoya bella has slender, upright branches that droop as they mature. Its leaves are small; white, ½-inch flowers with purple centers appear in tight clusters during the summer.

H. carnosa has 2 to 4-inch oval leaves and large clusters of creamy white flowers with five-pointed, pink stars in their centers. Its leaves are reddish when young. Several named varieties of *H. carnosa* may be available: 'Variegata', with whitish and pinkish edges around the leaves, and 'Compacta', with crinkly leaves closely spaced on short stems, are popular.

Grow hoyas in a sunny window in rich, heavy, well-drained soil. The plants bloom best when pot bound. Do not prune out the flowering wood; new blossom clusters form from stumps of old woody stems.

HUMATA TYERMANNII (Bear's foot fern). **House plant.** An indoor/outdoor plant, this small fern has furry, creeping rhizomes that look something like bear's feet. Fronds are 8 to 10 inches long and very finely cut, rising at intervals from the rhizomes. Like davallia in appearance and uses, humata is slower growing.

Gazania's *bold, daisylike flowers can bring bright masses of color to sunny locations.*

Almost sweeping the ground, *hedera ivy's long stems will add a casual grace to the patio.*

Plant combinations

By combining several different kinds of plants in a hanging container, you can create miniature landscapes. The possibilities are practically limitless. Just avoid combining plants that require different amounts of sun, shade, and moisture. The suggestions below should give you some ideas. In most cases, you needn't use all the plants listed in a combination. You may prefer to leave the perennial type plants, such as lotus and asparagus ferns, out of combinations involving mostly annual flowers. (Or save the perennials after the annuals have finished blooming.) Although a few of the plants below (marigolds and celosia, for example) aren't described in this book, they are fairly common. If you have questions about them, consult a nurseryman.

Here are sixteen suggested combinations:

1) In a basket, alternately plant blue lobelia, white sweet alyssum, yellow or gold dwarf marigolds. In a pot or box, set the marigolds in the center with alyssum or lobelia around the sides.

2) For a spring-blooming combination of rock garden plants, try a basket of purple aubrieta, yellow *Alyssum saxatile* (basket-of-gold), pink arabis, perennial candy-tuft (*Iberis gibraltarica*), with blue annual phlox (*Phlox drummondii*).

3) Blue petunias with yellow marigolds in a wire basket provide contrasting summer colors.

4) Violas or pansies go well with primroses in a wire basket or box. A small asparagus fern or two will give texture to the planting.

5) Try spring flowering schizanthus or nemesia (both have mixed colors) with asparagus or pellaea ferns.

6) White petunias, mixed nasturtiums, and pink sweet alyssum give good summer color. Lotus or ivy will provide foliage interest.

7) A sunloving spring combination is blue nierembergia, red convolvulus (*C. tricolor* 'Crimson Monarch'), and trailing African daisy (*Osteospermum fruticosum*).

8) For a lush arrangement in a shady spot, try begonias, primroses, and asparagus or pellaea ferns.

9) In a wire basket, plant red and gold plume or crested celosia (or red salvia) with blue ageratum and yellow marigolds. Use dwarf varieties of these plants.

10) Red verbena, dwarf snapdragons, and blue ageratum give bright summer color in a basket.

11) For a study in blues: violet petunias, dark blue ageratum, light blue lobelia (or add red impatiens for contrast).

12) Oxalis gives a nice mat of lush green beneath mimulus and other shade plants; later, oxalis sends up yellow flowers of its own.

13) Red impatiens and blue lobelia provide highlights for ivy or ferns.

14) A creation of foliage texture in a large basket: several varieties of ivy, *Artemisia* 'Silver Mound', lotus, and asparagus ferns.

15) Matlike baby's tears goes well with pellaea, asparagus ferns or ivy in a small pot.

16) Plant zebrina and tradescantia (wandering Jews) together in a pot.

Spidery group *of succulents: sedum with trailing stems and ice plant with pointed leaves.*

Cloverlike oxalis *engulfs this wire basket. Peeking out of it are grape ivy, begonia, and a fern.*

HYPOCYRTA nummularia (Goldfish plant). **House plant.** This plant has arching, 12-inch branches with neat pairs of shiny leaves. Its fat, tubular, 1-inch-long, orange flowers with pinched mouths resemble goldfish. Hypocyrta prefers the same treatment as its relative columnea (see page 51).

ICE PLANT. See Lampranthus and Oscularia.

IMPATIENS walleriana (Busy Lizzie). Often sold as *I. sultanii*. A perennial usually grown as an annual for summer color, impatiens has glossy, dark green leaves, 1 to 3 inches long, and is covered with 1 to 2-inch-wide flowers in summer. Flowers come in scarlet, pink, rose, violet, orange, or white and in some bicolors. Larger varieties may grow to as much as 2 feet tall; intermediate and dwarf types range from 4 to 12 inches. Use all but the tallest types. The stems will spill over the sides of a container as buds appear. Grow impatiens in partial shade and rich soil. Keep the soil moist. Grow plants from seeds or buy them as small plants from the nursery.

IPOMOEA purpurea (Morning glory). The common morning glory, grown for its showy, funnel-shaped, bell-like flowers, will spill nicely from a hanging container. Of the many named varieties, 'Heavenly Blue' has 4 to 5-inch, pure sky blue flowers with yellow throats, 'Pearly Gates' has white flowers and 'Scarlet O'Hara' has rosy red, scarlet-veined flowers. Grow them in the sun from seeds germinated in early spring. To speed germination, notch the seed coats with a sharp knife or soak them in warm water for 2 hours before planting. Plants require moderate watering; do not feed.

ITALIAN BELLFLOWER. See Campanula isophylla.

IVY. (See *Cissus rhombifolia*, grape ivy; *Cymbalaria muralis*, kenilworth ivy; *Hedera*, English and Algerian ivy; *Senecio mikanioides*, German ivy; *Plectranthus*, Swedish ivy.)

JAPANESE FELT FERN. See Pyrrosia.

JUNIPER. See Juniperus.

JUNIPERUS SPECIES. (Juniper). An unexpected hanging specimen is a juniper, perhaps trimmed and pruned to a bonsai form. The low, spreading varieties are best: *J. conferta*, shore juniper, that will tolerate heat; or *J. horizontalis* 'Wiltonii', blue carpet juniper, an intense silver blue and very low growing and spreading. Control growth and train the plants for form by pruning. Grow them in well-drained soil and full sun in cool-summer climates; in hot areas, provide partial shade. Don't let the soil become waterlogged.

KALANCHOE SPECIES. House plant. These are succulents. *K. manginii* is shrubby with thick, waxy leaves, olive green in color, on wiry branches. Terminal, orange red flowers at the ends of the stems are pendent. *K. uniflora* is creeping plant whose stems root at the joints. It has red flowers and fleshy, bright green leaves. Both are indoor/outdoor candidates that like good light or full sun.

KANGAROO VINE. See Cissus antarctica.

KENILWORTH IVY. See Cymbalaria.

The wax flower (Hoya bella) *produces clusters of star-like white flowers in the summertime.*

KITTEN'S EARS. See Cyanotis.

LAMPRANTHUS spectabilis (Trailing ice plant). A succulent subshrub, trailing ice plant has thick, gray green leaves on trailing stems. From March through May, the 2 to 2½-inch flowers are profuse, covering the stems to form a cascade of solid pink, rose pink, red, or purple color. Grow this ice plant in sun or light shade. Do not crowd the plants.

LANTANA. Often used as ground covers or as annual bedding plants, the shrubby, spreading varieties of lantana will trail and bush in hanging containers. They are excellent in full sun and in mild-winter climates will extend their normally long bloom period to the entire year.

The many named varieties are usually crosses between *L. montevidensis* and another species, *L. camara*. Several varieties with spreading growth are 'Carnival', with pink, yellow, crimson, and lavender flowers; 'Confetti', with yellow, pink, and purple flowers; 'Cream Carpet', with cream flowers having bright yellow throats; 'Gold Mound', with yellowish orange flowers; and 'Pink Frolic', pink and yellow flowers.

Prune lantana hard in spring to remove dead wood and to prevent woodiness. Water the plant thoroughly and let the soil dry out slightly before watering again; feed it lightly. Too much water and fertilizer reduce its bloom. Lantana tends to mildew in shade. Pinch stems regularly to stimulate fullness.

LATHYRUS odoratus (Sweet pea). The ever-favorite sweet pea comes in several bushy, low-growing types: Bijou, Knee-Hi, and bush forms. The plant's fragrant

Coleus

Episcia (*E. cupreata*)

Moneywort (*Lysimachia nummularia*)

Foliage is the main feature

With many plants foliage is the most striking feature. For instance, the leaf texture and rich green of full and bushy asparagus ferns account for their popularity, and the long, trailing stems and lush green leaves are an appeal of string of beads and moneywort.

But not all foliage is green. Try the prayer plant, whose leaves are marked in browns and reds; coleus, with its multitude of leaf colorations; and episcia, with creamy green foliage. Other suggestions for plants with foliage interest are listed in the special feature on page 51.

Prayer plant (*Maranta leuconeura*)

String of beads (*Senecio rowleyanus*)

Asparagus fern, Sprenger asparagus

flowers include almost every color imaginable. Grow sweet peas from seeds soaked in water for a few hours before planting to hasten germination, or from small nursery plants. Pinch out the tops of the plants several times to encourage strong side branching. Grow the plants in full sun but don't let the soil dry out. Cut the flowers frequently to keep new ones coming. Feed the plants regularly with a balanced fertilizer.

LIPSTICK PLANT. See Aeschynanthus lobbianus.

LOBELIA erinus. Lobelia will bloom from summer to frost, presenting a mass of small blue to violet (sometimes white or reddish purple) flowers. Both trailing and compact types are sold, and either is eminently suitable for hanging containers. The trailing types have longer cascading stems and include 'Hamburgia' (a light blue) and 'Sapphire' (a deep blue with white eyes). Compact varieties—such as 'Cambridge Blue', with clear, soft blue flowers and 'Crystal Palace', a rich, dark blue with bronzy leaves—will gently spill over the sides of a container. Lobelia is fine in combination with other flowering plants, such as violas, as well as with ferns and fibrous begonias. Grow them in moist, rich soil, in part shade.

LOBULARIA maritima (Sweet alyssum). A low-growing, branching, and easy perennial, alyssum is usually grown as an annual edging for borders. The flowers are small but appear in crowded clusters that form a carpet over the foliage. They are fine alone or with such flowers as dwarf marigolds. Grow the plants from seed or buy them in flats from the nursery. Many named varieties are available: 'Carpet of Snow' (2 to 4 inches tall) is white; 'Rosie O'Day' is a lavender pink; 'Royal Carpet' has rich violet purple flowers. All will gently spill or trail in hanging containers. Sweet alyssum prefers sun but takes light shade. It blooms in spring and summer in cold areas, year-round in mild areas.

LOROPETALUM chinense. A subtle plant, loropetalum has a neat, compact habit with tiered, arching, or drooping branches. The leaves are somewhat round and light green, about 1 to 2 inches long. An occasional leaf turns yellow or red throughout the growing season, adding a touch of color. Flowers are white or greenish white, forming in clusters at the ends of the branches. Each petal is attractively twisted. The heaviest bloom occurs in March and April. Grow the plant in full sun or partial shade in hot climates. It needs rich, well-drained soil and plenty of water.

LOTUS SPECIES. Both *Lotus berthelotii* (parrot's beak) and *L. mascaensis* have trailing stems thickly covered with handsome silver gray leaves, finely divided into narrow leaflets. *L. berthelotii* (perhaps the most often used) produces narrow, 1-inch-long scarlet blossoms in June and July. *L. mascaensis* is more spreading than trailing; it has yellow, ¾-inch flowers. Both are perennial but die back in cold weather. Trim the plants back occasionally to induce flat growth on *L. mascaensis* and to make *L. berthelotii* fuller and bushier. Grow both species in full or partial sun: good light is a must.

LYSIMACHIA nummularia (Moneywort; creeping Jennie). **House plant.** Moneywort is a hardy perennial with roundish, light green leaves neatly ordered in close pairs along trailing runners. A fine foliage plant, it also produces single, 1-inch yellow flowers at the leaf joints. Keep the soil moist. Outdoors, grow the plant in shade. Indoors, provide good light.

MADAGASCAR JASMINE. See Stephanotis.

MADAGASCAR PERIWINKLE. See Catharanthus.

MAHERNIA verticillata (Honey bell). A sun-loving perennial with finely divided, 1-inch-long leaves, honey bell produces somewhat straggly growth, with drooping stems. Yellow, bell-shaped, fragrant flowers appear in spring and bloom sporadically all year in mild climates. Keep dead flowers cut for the longest plant life.

MANDEVILLA SPECIES. House plant. *M.* 'Alice du Pont', an evergreen vine, is frequently grown as a house plant. Its leaves are 3 to 8 inches long, oval shaped, and dark green. Pink, 2 to 4-inch flowers appear in clusters among leaves from April through November. Grow the plant in a well-lighted window indoors or, during the warm season, outdoors in full sun in cool, humid areas; provide part shade in warm, dry climates. Pinch young plants to induce bushiness and to prevent scraggliness. Keep the soil moist.

Another species, Chilean jasmine (*M. laxa*), is a deciduous vine with 2 to 6-inch long oval leaves, heart-shaped at the base. Two-inch, trumpet-shaped flowers bloom in clusters during the summer; they have a strong, gardenialike fragrance. Grow the plant in rich soil and give full sun. Provide ample water.

MARANTA leuconeura (Prayer plant; rabbit tracks). **House plant.** A popular house plant with interestingly marked foliage, maranta features leafy stems, often spreading and generally less than 1 foot high. The leaves are 7 to 8 inches long by 3 to 4 inches wide on short stalks. The plant's attraction is its leaf coloring: green with streaks along the midrib and veins, and brown spots down each side (hence the name "rabbit tracks"). The leaves fold upward at night on some varieties, giving rise to the name "prayer plant." Several named varieties are available. 'Kerchoveana' has grayish leaves spotted with red on the underside. The leaves of 'Massangeana' are a rich purple on the underside. 'Erythroneura' is quite colorful, with velvety, olive-toned leaves traced red along the veins and tinged with a silvery streak down the center.

MARMALADE BUSH. See Streptosolen.

MEXICAN FLAME VINE. See Senecio confusus.

MIKANIA scandens. House plants. A perennial vine, mikania produces white or pink flowers from August through September in terminal heads and triangular leaves that are olive green with brownish veins on top and purplish underneath. This indoor/outdoor specimen likes a warm atmosphere, moist soil, and indirect light.

MIMULUS tigrinus (Monkey flower). A short-lived perennial usually grown as an annual for its spring and summer bloom, mimulus has smooth, succulent leaves and 2 to 2¼-inch yellow flowers splotched with brown and maroon. It's fine in a combination with ferns,

Large and spreading, *loropetalum is subtle rather than bold, with greenish white flowers and light, loose texture.*

Lotus, *or parrot's beak, has soft, gray green foliage and bright scarlet flowers.*

Mandevilla, *with its 2-4-inch pink summer flowers, is often grown as a house plant.*

Like tiny lanterns, *the reddish flowers of kalanchoe cover the fleshy, spreading stems.*

Ever-popular lantana *is a sunlover with profuse bloom; early in season, pinch stems to induce fullness.*

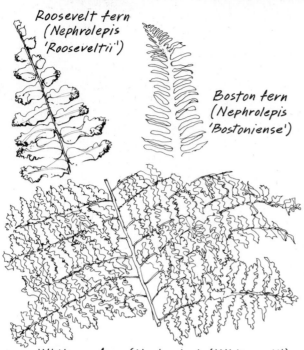

Roosevelt fern (Nephrolepis 'Rooseveltii')

Boston fern (Nephrolepis 'Bostoniense')

Whitman fern (Nephrolepis 'Whitmanii')

Sword fern: (Nephrolepis) *varieties: top left, 'Roose-veltii'; right, 'Bostoniense'; bottom, 'Whitmanii'.*

primroses, and tradescantia. Grow mimulus from seed or from small plants sold in the nursery during spring. Provide shade; keep the soil evenly moist.

MISTLETOE FIG. See Ficus diversifolia.

MONEYWORT. See Lysimachia.

MONKEY FLOWER. See Mimulus.

MORNING GLORY. See Ipomoea.

MYOPORUM parvifolium. Also known as *M. p.* 'Prostratum'. **House plant.** An evergreen, shrubby ground cover, myoporum has bright green, ½ to 1-inch leaves that densely cover the plant. White summer flowers, ½-inch wide, are followed by purple berries. Plants are low but spread quite extensively. Plant in moist soil in diffused sunlight. This is a house plant candidate.

MOSES-IN-THE-CRADLE. See Rhoeo.

NASTURTIUM. See Tropaeolum.

NEMESIA strumosa. Masses of ¾-inch, brilliantly colored flowers (with many bicolors and in every tone but green), 3 to 4 inches long on spreading spikes entirely cover these plants in late winter and spring. Use nemesia alone or with such plants as lobelia, viola, and small ferns. Nemesia prefers cool weather, part shade, and rich, moist soil. Pinch it to encourage bushiness.

NEPHROLEPIS exaltata (Boston ferns). **House plant.** With their lush, green fronds varying from light to dark green (depending on the variety), these are among the most popular and commonly grown ferns. Perhaps the best known is *N. e.* 'Bostoniense', the true Boston fern, which has spreading, arching fronds that will droop to

5 feet in favorable conditions with consistent care. The leaflets are undivided. Another variety, *N. e.* 'Rooseveltii', has dark green color. Leaflets are wavy around the margins and lobed at the tip. It is less trailing and has stiffer, more upright fronds than 'Bostoniense'. The variety 'Whitmanii' is fancier still than 'Rooseveltii'; each leaflet is divided into many smaller ones with deeply cut edges. 'Smithii'—very lacy—has broad, short fronds. 'Fluffy Ruffles' is upright with rich green, finely divided fronds.

Outdoors, these ferns like indirect light and require protection from frosts and from intense heat. Indoors, place them where they'll receive good light from a north or east window but no direct sun. Boston ferns prefer moisture and mild temperatures: a cool, humid room is better than a warm, dry one.

Keep the soil evenly moist; don't let it dry out. If the soil is light and fast draining, it's difficult to over water Boston ferns. (But don't let the plants soak in a drip saucer full of water.) Roots of Boston ferns like plenty of air; be sure to plant the fern in soil that is light and drains fast. For humidity, mist the foliage regularly (once or twice a day if the room or weather is especially hot and dry) with water from a sprayer.

NIEREMBERGIA hippomanica caerulea (Dwarf cup flower). A perennial with very branching, mounding growth, nierembergia will gently tumble over the sides of a container. The plants are covered all summer with 1-inch, blue to violet, bell-like flowers. Grow them in full sun.

ORCHID CACTUS. See Epiphyllum.

ORNITHOGALUM caudatum (Pregnant onion; false sea onion). **House plant.** The pregnant onion is a bulb grown indoors for its long, strap-shaped leaves that will hang down and trail to 5 feet. The small green and white flowers appearing on tall wands are less important. The bulb itself grows on the soil surface, not beneath it. Bulblets form under the skin and grow quite large before they drop and take root. Grow plants indoors in good light. Provide plenty of water. (If the bulb feels spongy, it's time to water; leaves drop off if soil is kept too dry for long periods.) Feed the plants once a month.

OSCULARIA deltoides (Ice plant). A low-growing subshrub with trailing branches, oscularia has thick, fleshy, triangular-shaped leaves—blue green with a pinkish flush. The purplish rose flowers, about ½ inch across, cover stems during late spring and early summer. Locate the plant in full sun and let the soil dry out slightly between waterings.

OSTEOSPERMUM fruticosum (Trailing African daisy). Producing winter and spring bloom in mild climates, trailing African daisy has 2-inch, daisylike flowers on long stems. Perennials often treated as annuals, the plants will bloom intermittently throughout the year in warm-winter regions. Grow them in full sun from seeds, cuttings, or nursery plants. Pinch tips of young plants to promote bushiness. Cut back old, sprawling branches to young side stems to keep the plants neat and to induce repeat bloom.

OXALIS SPECIES. House plant. Many species of oxalis have trailing or spreading stems with lush,

Bold red and white *spotted flowers are features of mimulus; grow it with shade plants.*

Pregnant onion (Ornithogalum) *is an unusual bulb planted on soil surface. Leaves are long and straplike.*

cloverlike leaves that make them attractive even without their lovely flowers. Grow them as house plants in a sunny window; summer-blooming types make attractive patio plants.

O. bowiei has pink or rose purple summer flowers, 1½ to 2 inches across, during the summer. *O. hirta*, with upright stems that gradually fall over from the weight of the leaves and flowers, blooms in late fall or winter; its flowers are bright rose pink and 1 inch wide. Plant it in the fall. *O. pes-caprae* has stems topped by clusters of 1-inch, bright yellow flowers that rise above cloverlike foliage in winter and spring.

PANSY. See Viola tricolor hortensis.

PARROT'S BEAK. See Lotus berthelotii.

PASSIFLORA SPECIES (Passion vine). Passiflora is often used in the garden against a trellis or wall, but you might try it in a hanging container. Trim the long stems to keep them neat and to maintain the length you want. The plant's flowers are intricately detailed. *P. caerulea*, blue crown passion flower, has greenish white flowers with a white and purple crown; the small fruits are orange. *P. edulis* (passion fruit) has three-lobed, deeply toothed, light green leaves; the 2-inch flowers are white with a white and purple crown. Spring and fall fruits are 3 inches long. *P. mollissima* has soft green foliage and long-tubed, pink to rose flowers 3 inches across. Its fruits are yellow and about 2 inches long. The plant likes full sun and warm nights and days.

PASSION VINE. See Passiflora.

PELARGONIUM SPECIES. Pelargoniums are frequently grown as summer annuals or house plants.

Several species have trailing stems. *P. domesticum*, or Lady Washington geraniums, have heart-shaped to kidney-shaped leaves that are dark green and 2 to 4 inches broad, with crinkled margins and toothed edges. The 2-inch flowers are quite showy, appearing in loose, rounded clusters in white and in shades of red, pink, lavender, and purple, some marked with darker colors. Choose branching and trailing varieties, such as 'Applause', 'Carisbrooke', 'Doris Firth', or 'South American Bronze'.

The common or garden geranium (*P. hortorum*) is a widely grown species that in some forms has strikingly colored leaves. Its flowers are single or double, slightly smaller than those of Lady Washington geraniums, and appear in clusters.

Ivy geranium (*P. peltatum*) trails to 2 or 3 feet. It has glossy, bright green, 2 to 3-inch, ivylike leaves with pointed lobes. White, pink, rose, red, and lavender flowers appear in rounded clusters. 'Mrs. Banks', with white, rose-marked flowers, is a good choice.

The scented-leaf geranium types, such as *P. tomentosum*, the peppermint-scented geranium that has small white flowers in fluffy clusters, might also be used as hangers.

Outdoors during the spring and summer, place geraniums in full sun or light shade in hot areas but never in dense shade. Indoors, give them a sunny window or the brightest location you can find. Geraniums bloom best when roots are slightly pot bound. Provide plenty of water. Pinch tip growth when plants are young to promote bushiness. Remove faded blooms regularly to promote new flowers. If you live in a harsh climate, take cuttings of your outdoor geraniums in the fall and root them in vermiculite or potting soil indoors during the winter.

Sunloving *trailing African daisy (Osteospermum) has long, loose stems covered with bold daisy flowers.*

One of many *trailing types of ice plant, oscularia forms a mass of foliage and bright flowers.*

PELLAEA rotundifolia (Roundleaf fern). Spreading, 1-foot-long fronds with evenly spaced, roundish leaflets about ¾-inch across characterize this fern. Grow it in partial shade; the plant is hardy to 24°. Since the plants are small, try them in a mixed basket or alone.

PEPEROMIA SPECIES. House plant. Peperomias are most often grown indoors as foliage plants. The trailing types are the best for hanging containers. *P. fosteri* has fleshy, dark green leaves, with lighter veins; *P. rotundifolia* features tiny, dark green, ¼-inch round leaves, often reddish underneath; *P. scandens* has leaves shaped like small hearts). *P. griseo-argentea* isn't really trailing, but has roundish, fleshy leaves on short floppy stems. (Plant it in a small decorative pot.)

Grow peperomias in north light, in cool or warm indoor temperatures. Use light, well-drained soil. Do not overwater; keep the soil slightly on the dry side.

PERIWINKLE. See Vinca.

PERNETTYA mucronata. An evergreen shrub with compact, clumpish growth, pernettya has leaves that are small, glossy, and dark green, giving it a fine-textured appearance. It develops tiny, white to pink, bell-shaped flowers in late spring, followed by colorful berries ½-inch across. Berry colors include white, pink, red, and purple. Grow it in acid, peaty soil with ample moisture. It takes full sun in cold-winter regions, partial shade where summers are long and hot.

PETUNIA. This favorite bedding plant should be pinched frequently during the early stages of growth to give it a bushy form that will spill thickly over the edges of a container. Varieties in the Cascade series ('White Cascade', for instance) have long, trailing stems, but they may still need some training and should be pinched to encourage branching.

The Cascade petunias belong to the Grandiflora class; other Grandifloras and varieties in the Multiflora class (which have smaller but more profuse flowers) can also be used. Choose sprawling, branching varieties that are not so short or compact that they won't spill. For mixed baskets of several different flowers, use small, compact types. Grow petunias in full sun. Late in the season cut back rangy plants by about half to stimulate new growth. Feed them monthly.

PHILODENDRON oxycardium. House plant. A number of the vinelike, small-leafed philodendrons will trail unless you give them a support to climb on. Try *P. oxycardium* (often sold as *P. cordatum*, a different plant). It has 5-inch, heart-shaped leaves that grow to 1 foot long on mature plants.

Grow philodendrons in rich, loose, well-drained soil and in good light but not in direct sun from a window. Provide ample water but keep the soil from becoming soggy. Feed the plants lightly and frequently for good growth and color.

PHLOX SPECIES. Trailing phlox (*P. nivalis*) is a perennial that grows in loose mats of narrow evergreen foliage producing big pink or white flowers in clusters during the late spring and early summer. Annual phlox (*P. drummondii*) has 6 to 18-inch erect stems with bright pastel flowers in close clusters at the top. Dwarf forms growing to about 6 inches fit well in mixed baskets. *P. subulata* is mat-forming to 6 inches high, with needlelike leaves. It has colorful, ¾-inch flowers

Staghorn fern *can grow against an organic surface such as moss, bark slab, or a tree trunk.*

Bright yellow flowers *of oxalis rise above plant's carpet of fresh, clover-shaped green leaves.*

in late spring and early summer. Grow phlox in full sun.

PIGGY-BACK PLANT. See Tolmiea.

PILEA SPECIES. House plant. *Pilea depressa*, one of the plants known as "baby's tears" (also see *Soleirolia*), is low and creeping, with many branches covered by small, round, ¼-inch leaves. Forming a dense mat that spills over the sides of a pot, it is a small plant that might best be used in a pot for a decorative indoor touch rather than for a main feature. It might also serve as a ground cover with other small house plants.

Pilea microphylla, the artillery plant, grows taller (from 6 inches to 1 foot) than *P. depressa* and has many spreading, twiggy branches. Its leaves are small. The plant's total effect is somewhat fernlike. Grow it as a house plant.

Pileas like porous soil, light shade or bright light, and temperatures of about 65° to 70°. Water the plants thoroughly, letting the soil surface dry out slightly before watering again. Feed the plants monthly with a complete fertilizer.

PLATYCERIUM SPECIES (Staghorn fern). The curious and unique staghorn fern, usually seen growing on bark slabs in the light shade of a patio or lanai roof in warm-winter gardens, is a tropical epiphytic fern. (Epiphytic plants do not grow in soil but attach themselves to a tree trunk or branch and send out aerial roots.)

Staghorn ferns have two kinds of fronds: sterile and fertile. The sterile ones are flat and pale green, aging to tan and brown. They cling to a surface (such as a tree limb or bark slab), supporting the plant and collecting organic matter and water to provide nutrients and

moisture. The fertile fronds are long and spread outward from the sterile ones. They are forked and divided, giving the plants an appearance of deer or moose antlers. The ferns are not common, but you may find several species in nurseries in warm, temperate climates.

P. bifurcatum is quite hardy to 20° to 22°, with only a lath or patio roof for protection. Its fertile fronds are clustered and reach 3 feet in length; it forms numerous offsets that can be used for propagation. *P. grande* needs protection from frosts and resents overwatering. It is difficult to grow in humid climates.

Plant the staghorn fern by wiring it to a redwood board with a pad of moss or other coarse organic matter underneath, forming a pocket that will hold water and fertilizer. Or wire the plant to a tree limb if frosts are rare and the location is warm and protected. In time, the roots of the plant will take hold. Don't let copper or galvanized wire touch the plant's roots: pad wire with moss to protect the plant.

Provide plenty of water to the moss pocket behind the plant but don't keep the moss soggy. Feed frequently and continuously. Bring plants indoors for winter protection.

PLECTRANTHUS SPECIES (Swedish ivy; creeping Charlie). **House plant.** Usually grown for its trailing stems covered with thick, scalloped-edged leaves, plectranthus thrives in low or medium-light intensity. You may find two species: *P. australis* has shiny, dark green leaves; *P. oertendahlii* has leaves with silvery-marked veins and purplish, scalloped margins. Both are fairly easy and grow rapidly. Be careful not to over water; this causes leaves to fade, lose their crisp feel and appearance, and eventually turn brown. Keep the

Tuberous begonia 'Pendula'

Begonias and fuchsias–they're naturals

Spectacular in the air are begonias and fuchsias. Their luscious flowers take many captivating forms and colors. However, both plants have climate preferences for humidity and moderate temperatures. Talk to a nurseryman to see if types adapted to your area are available. Usually named for their flower color, tuberous begonias of the 'Pendula' variety feature long, pendent stems and large blooms. Also try bushy fibrous begonia types. Fuchsias grow in all forms and sizes. For hanging, you'll want varieties with trailing stems, such as 'Marinka', 'Swingtime', and 'First Love'.

Fibrous begonia

Tuberous begonia 'Pendula': flower detail

Fuchsia 'Marinka'

Fuchsia 'First Love'

Fuchsia 'Swingtime': flower detail

soil slightly dry. The stiff, succulent stems may break easily.

PLUMBAGO auriculata. Often sold as *P. capensis*. In the garden, plumbago is a large, sprawling, and mounding bush. But in hanging containers, the plants can easily be trained and pruned into a bushy clump that is covered from March through December with clusters of white to light blue, 1-inch, phloxlike flowers. (Plumbago has a year-round bloom in frost-free climates.) It takes full sun, but in very hot desert areas the intense sun may bleach the flower color. Plant it in well-drained soil.

PODOCARPUS gracilior. Use cutting-grown specimens, often sold as *P. elongatus*. Podocarpus grown from cuttings have long, limber branches covered with bluish gray leaves. When young, the plants can be trained to droop if weights are attached to the ends of the stems. Two or three hanging specimens create a willowy and graceful effect, with the branches arching gently. The plants are slow growing. After six months or so, you can remove the weights; the stems will continue drooping by themselves. Occasionally thin the plant by pruning out renegade upright-growing branches. Place the plant in partial sun or in light shade in very hot summer areas.

POLYGONUM capitatum. A tough, evergreen perennial, polygonum grows only 6 inches high but trails extensively. Its leaves are about 1½ inches long: new ones have a dark green color; older ones are tinged pink. The pink flowers have a long blooming period—throughout the year in mild climates. Polygonum combines well in a wire basket with white sweet alyssum (see *Lobularia*, page 62) and lobelia (see page

62). The leaves die or discolor in temperatures below about 28°. Grow the plant in full sun. Keep soil moist.

POLYPODIUM SPECIES. The polypodium ferns are a wide and variable group, but all like partial or filtered shade.

Hare's foot fern (*P. aureum*) is large, with heavy, brown, creeping rhizomes eventually covering the surfaces of a basket. It sends out coarse, 3 to 5-foot fronds that may drop in light frost but will quickly come back.

P. coronans has leathery, dark green fronds that are 2 to 4 feet long and uncut or scalloped near the base but coarsely cut above. An epiphyte, it attaches itself to a flat organic surface, such as a tree limb or board. Plant and grow it as you would a staghorn fern (see *Platycerium*).

The licorice fern (*P. vulgare*) is large and somewhat coarse. Native California varieties tend to summer dormancy unless they're given plenty of water. European varieties are evergreen. Grow the licorice fern in leaf mold or other organic matter.

PORTULACA grandiflora (Rose moss). Portulaca is a low-growing annual with spreading, trailing stems and roselike double or single flowers in red, cerise, rose pink, orange, yellow, white, and pastel shades. The flowers open fully only in the sun, closing in the late afternoon and on cloudy days.

PRAYER PLANT. See Maranta.

PREGNANT ONION. See Ornithogalum.

PRIMROSE. See Primula.

PRIMULA SPECIES (Primrose). Two primula species might be used in hanging containers. Fairy primrose

Off come the weights *that helped train the branches of this podocarpus to grow outwards and down.*

A giant sphere *is created by fronds of mature pyrrosia fern that engulfs a wire basket.*

(*P. malacoides*) is usually grown as an annual for spring or fall bloom. It has ½ to ¾-inch flowers in large, lacy clusters along delicate stems rising above the foliage. The colors are pink, white, lavender, and reddish purple. Massed in a box or pot, the plants tend to spill over the sides of a container.

Polyanthus, or English primrose (*P. polyantha*), has 1 to 2-inch flowers in clusters at the tops of upright stems. The leaves are full and lush, growing in tight, basal clumps. Use the miniature or dwarf types in mixed-basket plantings or plant them with young ferns. Both types do best in part or light shade, cool weather, and moist soil.

PURPLE HEART. See Setcreasea.

PYRROSIA lingua (Japanese felt fern). Growing from creeping root stalks, the dark green, undivided, lance-shaped fronds of this distinctive fern will eventually cover an entire basket. The fronds reach 15 inches in length and have a feltlike texture. Grow pyrrosia in shade; keep the soil evenly moist.

QUAMOCLIT sloteri (Cardinal climber). This is an annual vine with tubular flowers that flare outward at the mouth into a five-lobed star. The flowers are occasionally white but most often red. Pinch the plants to keep them neat and to promote branching. They need full sun.

QUEEN'S TEARS. See Billbergia.

RABBIT TRACKS. See Maranta.

RHAPHIDOPHORA aurea. Often sold as *Scindapsus aureus*. **House plant.** A house plant related to and resembling climbing philodendrons, rhaphidophora has oval, leathery green leaves 2 to 4 inches long. Give

Large, coarse, *and spreading fronds of* Polypodium coronans *require space for good display.*

it the same care that you would a philodendron. The variety 'Marble Queen' has leaves streaked with yellow. The plants, especially young specimens, may be shown off best in a small, attractive clay pot.

RHIPSALIDOPSIS gaertneri (Easter cactus). **House plant.** The Easter cactus, like the Christmas cactus (*Schlumbergera bridgesii*), is a fine plant for indoor color. In warm-winter climates, it can be grown outdoors on a protected patio in light or partial shade. Its growth is spreading, with drooping, arching, jointed branches that are flattish, bright green, smooth, and spineless. Flowers to 3 inches long are upright or horizontal, appearing in April and May, sometimes again in September. Many varieties in shades of red and pink are available. Grow them in a well-lighted window; use rich, porous soil with plenty of leaf mold and sand. (The plants will tolerate some sun.) Though true cactus, rhipsalidopsis (and schlumbergera) are jungle, not desert, natives. Keep soil moist and feed regularly.

RHIPSALIS paradoxa. House plant. Rhipsalis is a cactus with spineless, jointed stems, three-sided and branching, that may dangle to 3 feet. The flower clusters are white. Grow the plant in moist soil indoors in a well-lighted window.

RHOEO spathacea (Moses-in-the-cradle). **House plant.** Rhoeo is not truly trailing. Instead, it has leaf tufts 6 to 12 inches wide, with a dozen or so broad, arching, sword-shaped leaves that spread out over the edge of a container. The leaves are dark green on top and purplish underneath. The variety 'Vittata' has striped red and yellowish green leaves. The flowers are small and white, with three petals; they're crowded into boat-shaped bracts borne down among the leaves. Most often grown as a house plant, rhoeo will take low or high light intensity. But you can try it in a protected location outdoors.

RHOICISSUS capensis (Evergreen grape). **House plant.** Often sold as *Cissus capensis*. A tough vine, evergreen grape is often grown as a house plant for its roundish to kidney-shaped, scalloped-edged leaves that appear much like the leaves of the true grape. It can be grown outdoors if the climate is moderate. Indoors, it takes low as well as high light intensity. Be sure to water it regularly. Outdoors, the plants will tolerate full sun if its roots are kept cool and moist.

ROCKCRESS. See Arabis.

ROSARY VINE. See Ceropegia.

ROSE MOSS. See Portulaca.

ROSEMARY. See Rosmarinus.

ROSMARINUS officinalis (Rosemary). This is an aromatic herb with glossy, dark green, narrow leaves that are grayish white on the underside. Its flowers—bluish violet—cover plants like a blanket in spring and occasionally throughout the summer. The leaves can be used as a food seasoning. Its growth form is ruggedly picturesque. Low-growing varieties, such as *R. o.* 'Prostratus', (dwarf rosemary) and *R. o.* 'Lockwood de Forest', are best for hanging. Although the plants endure hot sun, part sun or even thin shade dappled with sun suit them well. Be sure to use well-drained soil. Keep the soil slightly on the dry side; excess feeding and watering result in rank growth and woodiness. Control growth and plant form by pinching tips when the plants are small.

ROUNDLEAF FERN. See Pellaea.

SANDWORT. See Arenaria.

SAXIFRAGA stolonifera (Strawberry geranium; Saxifrage). **House plant.** Strawberry geranium is a popular house or patio plant, having a creeping form and roundish, white-veined leaves to 4 inches across. One-inch flowers are white and grow in loose, open clusters. Outdoors, it likes shade (light shade or part sun in cool areas). Indoors, grow the plants in a well-lighted window. Keep the soil moist.

SAXIFRAGE. See Saxifraga.

SCHIZANTHUS pinnatus (Poor man's orchid). This is an annual with small, orchidlike flowers having vari-colored markings on pink, rose, lilac, purple, or white backgrounds. The effect is a mass of lively color. The stems, slightly trailing or drooping, spill over the sides of shallow containers enough to cover them. Best used for spring color in filtered shade and cool regions, the plants must be protected from frost and heat. Since they're slow to sprout from seeds, buy them in flats from the nursery or start them from seeds sown in fall. Combine them with such flowers as fairy primrose (see *Primula malacoides*) or use them alone.

SCHIZOCENTRON elegans (Spanish shawl). Spanish shawl is a tender perennial with a creeping, vinelike habit. Its ½-inch-wide leaves are oval, with three distinctly marked veins: the leaves and stems turn red as the season advances. Summer flowers, 1 inch wide and magenta in color, appear among the leaves in summer. The plant prefers a shady location.

SCHLUMBERGERA bridgesii (Christmas cactus). Often sold as *Zygocactus*. **House plant.** December flowers, rosy purple red, many petaled, and tubular to 3 inches long, are the main feature of this spineless cactus usually grown as a house plant. The arching, drooping branches are jointed and flattish, spreading 2 to 3 feet when well grown. Plant Christmas cactus in a rich, porous soil with plenty of leaf mold and sand. Water the plant frequently and feed it regularly with liquid fertilizer (light doses as often as once a week). Indoors, provide a sunny or well-lighted window. If you live in a warm-winter area, grow the plant on a protected patio in half shade.

SCINDAPSUS. See Rhaphidophora.

SEDUM SPECIES (Includes donkey tail). A host of sedums have long, trailing stems, fascinating growth habit, and/or attractive flowers. Most are succulents with fleshy leaves.

S. lineare, with its star-shaped, yellow flowers in late spring and early summer, spreads vigorously. Its stems are closely set, with narrow, 1-inch-long, light green leaves.

S. morganianum, popularly called "donkey tail," has trailing stems that may grow to 3 or 4 feet long in six to

Vertical planters

This mural is alive with small succulents. It consists of a wooden box with chicken wire stretched across the front. Construct the box frame with redwood 2 by 4s, nailed or screwed together. The frame can be any dimensions you like, but remember that large boxes can be very heavy. This one measures 4 feet by 1 foot 8 inches.

Attach lightweight cedar boards to the frame's back. With the box lying face up on the ground, pour in light potting soil. Fill it so soil won't shift and settle when box is tilted. Cover soil with ½-inch-thick layer of moss. Stretch 1-inch mesh chicken wire over the moss, tacking it to the box sides. Use wood facing strips to hide the wire edges.

Plant the box with such low-growing succulents as small aeoniums, crassulas, echeverias, sedums, sempervivums, and other mat-forming, rosette types. Use cuttings rather than full-grown plants; poke the stem ends through the wire and moss and into dry soil. Don't water until roots form. When plants take root, hang the mural against a wall. Water it through holes drilled in the top 2 by 4.

Collage *of succulents grows in shallow 2 by 4 box. Chicken wire and moss keep soil from spilling out.*

eight years. Thick, gray green, tubelike leaves surround the stem, overlapping each other to create a distinctive braided or ropelike texture and appearance. The flowers are insignificant. An indoor plant everywhere, it can be grown outside in a protected location in mild climates if given half or partial shade. Grow it in fast-draining soil, protect it from wind, water it freely, and feed it two or three times during the summer with a liquid fertilizer. Start the plant from cuttings taken from the ends of mature stems.

S. sieboldii is attractive with or without its pink autumn flowers, which appear in large, dense clusters at the ends of spreading, trailing, unbranched stems. Groups of three flattish leaves along the stems give it a distinctive texture.

S. spathulifolium has spoon-shaped, blue green leaves tinged reddish purple and packed into rosettes on short, trailing stems. Bright yellow flowers appear in spring and summer.

S. stahlii is twiggy and trailing, with small, bean-shaped, dark green, brown-tinged leaves and yellow flowers in autumn or summer.

SELENICEREUS macdonaldiae (Queen of the night). **House plant.** This is a relatively spineless cactus, with long jointed and trailing stems, glossy dark green and tinged purple in color. The night blooming flowers are quite showy. Grow it as a house plant in good strong light. Keep the soil evenly moist but not soaking wet.

SENECIO SPECIES. Relatives of the daisy, senecio species are suitable for hanging. They include a variety of rather diverse plants, ranging from bushy growers with seasonal color to succulent trailers.

A tender vine, *stephanotis grows indoors or out. Flowers are fragrant with waxy white color.*

Mexican flame vine (*S. confusus*) is an evergreen or deciduous vine. In cold climates it is frequently grown as an annual. Its branches are cascading, with flaming orange daisylike flower clusters at the ends. Grow it in sun or light shade. Keep the soil moist.

German ivy (*S. mikanioides*) is a perennial vine with fleshy, ivy-shaped leaves on long, trailing stems; it's usually grown indoors.

String of beads (*S. rowleyanus*) is a succulent with slow-growing, thin, trailing stems 6 to 8 feet long. The stems are crowded with ½-inch, spherical, green leaves that resemble beads. The flowers are small, white, and have a carnation scent. Locate the plant indoors in good light or outside in partial shade and a protected location; it's hardy to 25°.

SETCREASEA purpurea (Purple heart). **House plant.** An indoor/outdoor plant with leaning or arching stems, setcreasea has leaves that are narrowly oval with a strong purple shade, particularly underneath. Related to the wandering Jews (tradescantia and zebrina), it may be sold under that name. Although it takes light shade, its color is best in the sun. Plants may be unattractive in the wintertime.

SHRIMP PLANT. See Beloperone.

SNOW-IN-SUMMER. See Cerastium.

SOLEIROLIA soleirolii (Baby's tears, angel's tears). **House plant.** Often sold as *Helxine soleirolii*. Soleirolia is a creeping perennial with small, roundish leaves that form a lush green mat only 1 to 4 inches high, spilling gently over the edges of a container. It's grown indoors or out in shade, or full sun in cool regions if given ample water. Use it alone in a small, decorative container or as a filler or ground cover with mixed baskets of shade and moisture-loving ferns or flowers.

SOLLYA fusiformis (Australian bluebell creeper). Clusters of ½-inch-long, brilliant blue, bell-shaped flowers cover this loose, downward spilling shrub during the summer. Grow it in full sun in moderate areas, in part shade in warm-summer regions. It likes moisture but needs good drainage.

SPANISH SHAWL. See Schizocentron.

SPIDER PLANT. See Chlorophytum.

SQUIRREL'S FOOT FERN. See Davallia.

STAGHORN FERN. See Platycerium.

STAR JASMINE. See Trachelospermum.

STEPHANOTIS floribunda (Madagascar jasmine). **House plant.** Stephanotis is an indoor/outdoor plant, with glossy green leaves to 4 inches long and white, fragrant, funnel-shaped flowers that bloom in open clusters in June when grown outdoors. Outdoors, it does best in warm, light shade. Ideally, the roots should be in shade, the plant itself in filtered sun. Feed and water it liberally. Before bringing the plant indoors, let the soil dry out slightly. Indoors, grow stephanotis in bright light, away from direct sun.

STRAWBERRY. See Fragaria.

STRAWBERRY GERANIUM. See Saxifraga.

STREPTOSOLEN jamesonii (Marmalade bush). **House plant.** Streptosolen is a viny shrub often grown as an indoor/outdoor plant in cold areas. Ribbed, oval, 1½-inch leaves and yellow to brilliant orange, 1-inch flowers appear in loose clusters from April through October. Grow the plant in a warm spot. Use quick-draining soil and provide ample water. The plant needs protection from frosts and from the hottest sun.

STRING-OF-BUTTONS. See Crassula perfossa.

STRING OF BEADS. See Senecio rowleyanus.

STRING OF HEARTS. See Ceropegia.

SWEDISH IVY. See Plectranthus.

SWEET ALYSSUM. See Lobularia.

SWEET PEA. See Lathyrus.

SYNGONIUM podophyllum. House plant. A philodendron relative with long stalks, this plant has arrow-shaped, dull green leaves that are sometimes lobed. It is an easy house plant, requiring conditions similar to the philodendron. There are many named varieties with colorful leaf markings.

TETRASTIGMA SPECIES. This is an evergreen vine grown for its glossy, dark green leaves up to 1 foot across and divided fanlike into three to five oval leaflets with toothed edges. Its growth is somewhat like grape ivy (*Cissus rhombifolia*). Plants can grow quite large: use young specimens.

T. voinierianum is a fast grower. New leaves are covered with thick fuzz.

T. vomerensis is slower growing. New growth is covered with orange brown fuzz that lingers on the undersides of leaves to contrast with the rich green of mature leaves.

Ideally, the roots should be shaded and the plant allowed to spread out into the sun. Grow it in warm, well-lighted shade in a container that will keep the roots cool. Provide plenty of water.

THUNBERGIA SPECIES. Black-eyed Susan vine (*T. alata*) is a perennial usually grown as an annual for its flaring, tubular, 1-inch-wide flowers in orange, yellow, or white—all with purple black throats. Grow it in sun and pinch and trim it to keep the vinelike stems bushy and full. Two other species are *T. gibsonii* and *T. gregorii*. Both are perennial vines grown as annuals. They have flaring, tubelike flowers, mostly orange, appearing singly at the ends of short stems. Grow both in full sun.

THYMUS SPECIES. (Thyme). Many species of thyme (an herb whose leaves are frequently used as a food seasoning) are low growing and spreading or gently mounding.

T. herba-barona (caraway-scented thyme) forms a thick mat of dark green, ¼-inch leaves with a caraway fragrance.

Woolly thyme (*T. lanuginosus*) grows in a 2 to 3-inch-high mat of small gray, woolly leaves.

Mother-of-thyme, or creeping thyme (*T. serpyllum*), grows to 6 inches high in a spreading mat. Silver thyme, a variety of mother-of-thyme, has leaves variegated with silver. Lemon thyme, another variety of

A giant vine *with huge leaves, tetrastigma is best grown in containers when young.*

mother-of-thyme, has yellow variegated leaves and is scented with a lemony fragrance.

The common thyme (*T. vulgaris*) grows more upright (to 1 foot high) but may lean over the edges of a container.

Grow thyme in full or part sun. Keep it in shape by pinching the stems. You might hang thyme from the kitchen porch, where you can pick the leaves for cooking. Or plant it up with other herbs to create an herb garden in the air. (See page 10.)

TOLMIEA menziesii (Piggy-back plant). **House plant.** The piggy-back plant is a house plant grown for its bright green leaves (to 5 inches across) and its attractive growth of new leaves on shortish stems rising from the centers of old leaves. Propagate the plants by pinching off leaves and setting them in water so that the stems and leaf junctions are submerged. Roots will quickly sprout, and new leaves will grow from leaf center. Pot the leaf as soon as roots form. This plant likes good light and moist soil; feed it regularly.

TOMATO, SMALL FRUITED VARIETIES (*Lycopersicom esculentum*). Cherry tomatoes make unusual hanging container plants. In addition to presenting a lush cascade of foliage, they will be quite a conversation piece when the fruits ripen. Plant tomatoes in spring when small plants become available at the nursery. Many varieties are available; your nursery should carry those most suited to your climate. Make certain to get small-fruited or cherry varieties, such as 'Red Cherry' and 'Tiny Tim'. After planting them in your container, gradually expose the plants to more and more sun each week until they will stand direct sun all day without wilting. Water them frequently—perhaps daily during hot spells. If the stems don't seem to trail at first, try training them gently with

Piggy-back plants (Tolmiea) *send out new leaves from centers of mature ones, creating unique texture.*

Cherry tomatoes *in a hanging pot or box offer tasty hors d'oeuvres on a terrace, patio, or deck.*

weights (see page 40) or wait until the stems grow longer and the fruits pull them downward.

TORENIA fournieri (Wishbone flower). This is a compact, bushy annual, with gloxinialike flowers in light blue marked with deeper blue and with bright yellow throats. White forms are also available. The stamens are arranged in a configuration resembling a wishbone. Torenia blooms during the summer and fall; stems will tumble over the edges of a container. Where summers are cool and short, grow torenia in full sun. In warmer areas, grow them in part shade.

TRACHELOSPERMUM jasminoides (Star jasmine). If you cut back upright stems and tip pinch to encourage bushiness and control growth, fragrant star jasmine will spread and droop in a hanging container. The star-shaped flowers, about 1 inch across and a lovely white color, bloom profusely in small clusters on short side branches in June and July and have a delicate fragrance. They contrast brightly with the dark green leaves. Grow star jasmine in a warm location and in part or filtered sun.

TRADESCANTIA fluminensis (Wandering Jew). **House plant.** One of a number of plants commonly known as wandering Jew (zebrina, cyanotis, setcreasea, and tripogandra also may occasionally be sold as wandering Jew), this popular and easy house plant has long, trailing stems with swollen joints where 2½-inch-long oval or oblong leaves are attached. The common form has dark green leaves; the leaves of the frequently sold variety 'Variegata' are light green striped with yellow or white. The flowers are white but not showy. Grow the plant indoors in good light. In warm areas, grow it as an indoor/outdoor plant on a protected patio in filtered or light shade.

TRIPOGANDRA multiflora (Bridal veil). **House plant.** Bridal veil, also known as Tahitian bridal veil, is related to the common wandering Jews: *Tradescantia fluminensis* and zebrina. (In fact, it frequently is sold under the name wandering Jew.) It is a very branching plant with thin, wiry stems (more slender than the other wandering Jews), covered with olive green leaves that are narrowly ovular with pointed tips. The undersides of leaves are purplish. Summer flowers are white and tiny, appearing in clusters.

Like tradescantia and zebrina, bridal veil is an indoor/outdoor plant that prefers good indirect light or filtered shade, moderately warm temperatures, and needs protection from chilly weather. Pinch it back regularly to encourage bushiness. Keep the soil moist but not soaking wet.

TROPAEOLUM majus (Nasturtium). Perennials usually grown as annuals for spring and summer flowers, nasturtiums come in two basic forms: climbing types that will trail to some length and dwarf types that grow in a compact bush, spilling over the edges of a container in a thick clump. Both types have round, shield-shaped leaves on longish stalks and bold fragrant flowers in maroon, red brown, orange, yellow, and red through creamy white tones, some with mixed colors. Grow nasturtiums in full or partial sun from seeds sown in early spring. For maximum bloom, fertilize sparingly and keep the plants on the dry side.

VELVET PLANT. See Gynura.

VERBENA SPECIES. Both garden verbena (V. *hybrida*) and Peruvian verbena (V. *peruviana*) are perennials usually grown as annuals. They thrive in sun and heat. Summer flowers appear in flat, compact clusters that lavishly cover the low, branching, and spreading

Hyacinths (right), primroses (left)

Black-eyed Susan vine (*Thunbergia alata*)

Fun with hanging plants

The very idea of plants in the air opens the door to fun and frivolity. You should feel free to try many different plants and plant combinations. Bulbs, for example, needn't always be earthbound—nor does a bonsai——just look at the hyacinths and cedar shown here. (Also see special features on pages 9 and 14.)

Unleash your imagination and try incorporating items like an antique ox yoke into your ensemble. Or suspend containers one above the other to create arrangements like that shown above.

Combinations of plants create landscapes in miniature. As shown in the wire wall basket (facing page, bottom right), you can use anything from ferns to bedding plants. (See special feature, page 58.)

Bonsai cedar with moss

Italian bellflower (*Campanula isophylla*)

Alyssum, ferns, begonias, lobelia

stems. Colors run from whites and pinks to reds and blues, with some mixed tones. Many named varieties are sold. Water early in the day to avoid mildew.

VINCA SPECIES (Periwinkle). Tough, easy-to-grow perennials, vincas come in two trailing species (for *Vinca rosea* see *Catharanthus roseus*). *Vinca major* has long, trailing stems covered with oval, glossy, dark green leaves (one variety variegated with white) and 1 to 2-inch, lavender blue, flattish flowers on the ends of short branches growing from the main stems.

Vinca minor (dwarf periwinkle) is similar in almost every way to *V. major* except that it is smaller, having closely spaced flowers on short stems. The leaves are oblong.

VIOLA SPECIES (Pansy; violet). The ever-popular violas (*V. cornuta*) and pansies (*V. tricolor hortensis*) are excellent for spring and early summer color. Massed alone in a pot or a box or used with other spring flowers or small ferns in a mixed basket, they'll give a fine display of lively color. Both violas and pansies are perennials usually grown as annuals and bought from the nursery in flats. The main differences between them are in growth form and color. Pansies are somewhat larger and have a more spreading habit than violas. Violas usually have clear, solid colors (sometimes finely marked in contrasting colors), whereas pansies are generally bicolored, with strong markings in the center. They require similar conditions and treatment: rich, moist soil and protection from the hottest sun. Feed and water violas and pansies regularly.

A third viola species is the Australian violet (*V. hederacea*), which has a tufted, spreading habit, kidney-shaped leaves, and flowers ¼ to ¾ inch across in the summer.

WISHBONE FLOWER. See Torenia.

WANDERING JEW. See Tradescantia and Zebrina. Also see *Cyanotis, Setcreasea,* and *Tripogandra*.

WAX FLOWER, WAX PLANT. See Hoya.

WOOD FERN. See Dryopteris.

XYLOSMA congestum. A loose, graceful, spreading shrub that will grow quite tall if left alone, but will spread and trail if you prune the mainstem to keep growth low. Side branches grow long and arch or droop over container sides. Plants are heat tolerant, grow best in full sun or filtered shade.

ZEBRINA pendula (Wandering Jew). **House plant.** Zebrina is a house plant with much the same habit and general appearance (and even the same common name) as *Tradescantia fluminensis*. Its variegated leaf forms are popular. 'Quadricolor' has purplish green leaves with bands of white, pink, and carmine red. Types with variegated leaves need more light (in order to develop good color) than single-color types. Try combining zebrina and tradescantia in the same pot for a colorful foliage effect. Grow them in good light indoors or outdoors. During the summer, grow them outdoors in filtered or in light shade and a protected location.

ZYGOCACTUS. See Schlumbergera.

Pretty nasturtiums *are as appealing in hanging containers as they are in a garden flower bed.*

Tiny white flowers *give tripogandra (or Tahitian bridal veil) a lacy, delicate texture.*

Index

Boldface numbers refer to photographs

Photographers

William Aplin: 6; 12 bottom; 43 all; 45 all; 47; 54; 63 center left; 67 left; 68 bottom left; 70 left; 72, 73; 74; 77 top. **George J. Ball, Inc.:** 13 bottom; 52 top; 53 top left and right; 76 right. **Glenn Christiansen:** 7 top right; 11; 56; 65 right. **Richard Dawson:** 67 right. **Richard Fish:** 7 left center and bottom right; 13 top right; 15 bottom right; 21 right; 76 left; 77 bottom right. **Gerald R. Fredrick:** 10. **Jeannette Grossman:** 48. **Eda Johnstone:** 66 right. **Ells Marugg:** 4 all; 5; 12 top; 13 top left; 14; 15 top right; 17; 19 all; 20 all; 21 top and bottom left; 23 all; 25 all; 26 all; 28–31 all; 35; 41 right; 42; 49 all; 50 bottom; 52 bottom; 53 bottom left and right; 58 top; 60–61 all; 63 top left, bottom left and right; 68 top and bottom right; 69 all; 70 right; 77 bottom left; 78 right. **Don Normark:** 7 top left; 15 top left; 50 top; 57 left; 58 bottom; 66 left; 75. **Ron Partridge:** 63 top right. **Norman A. Plate:** 7 bottom left. **Darrow M. Watt:** 15 center left; 41 left; 57 right; 59; 65 left; 71; 78 left. **Doug Wilson:** 15 bottom left.